ICB Bookkeeping
Levels I & II

Practical
Bookkeeping

Kit

KAPLAN
PUBLISHING

British Library Cataloguing-in-Publication Data

A catalogue record for this book is available from the British Library.

PUBLISHED BY:

Kaplan Publishing UK
Unit 2 The Business Centre
Molly Millars Lane
Wokingham
RG41 2QZ

ISBN 978-1-84710-919-4

KEY TECHNIQUES QUESTION BANK CONTENTS

Workbook Preface

This workbook has been written for levels I & II of the Institute of Certified Bookkeepers (ICB) levels I & II Manual route syllabus.

It is designed to compliment the corresponding ICB study text (Practical Bookkeeping) which contains the detailed syllabus coverage. The chapters in this workbook relate exactly to the study text chapters and are designed to consolidate knowledge.

KAPLAN PUBLISHING

Key Technique Questions

Chapter 1
Double entry bookkeeping – introduction

QUESTION 1

Bertie Wooster started a business as an antique dealer on 1 July 20X7.

Required

Show the accounting equation which results from each of the following transactions made during Bertie's first two weeks of trading.

(a)   Started the business with £5,000 in cash as opening capital.
(b)   Bought an Edwardian desk for £500 cash.
(c)   Bought 5 art deco table lamps for £200 each, on credit from Roderick Spode.
(d)   Sold the desk for £750 cash.
(e)   Sold 4 of the table lamps for £300 each on credit to his Uncle Tom.
(f)   Paid rent of £250 cash.
(g)   Drew £100 in cash out of the business for living expenses.
(h)   Earned £50 for writing a magazine article, but had not yet been paid for it.
(i)   Paid Roderick Spode £500 on account.
(j)   Received £1,200 from Uncle Tom in full settlement of the amount due.
(k)   Bought a van for use in the business for £4,000 cash.
(l)   Received a telephone bill for £150 but did not pay it yet.

Note: Each transaction follows on from the one before.

QUESTION 2

On 1 January 20X6 Esmond Haddock inherited £3,000 from an aunt and decided to open his own sports equipment shop. During January the following transactions took place.

01 January	Paid the £3,000 into a bank account
02 January	Paid one month's rent of £100 for the shop premises
10 January	Bought stock of sports equipment for £1,000 cash
14 January	Paid £50 for display equipment
30 January	Drew out £150 for his own use
31 January	Bought sports equipment on credit for £1,500

During the month he sold for £830 half of the equipment he purchased on 10 January. £800 was received in cash and £30 was owed to him by one customer.

Required

Show the accounting equation of the business at 31 January 20X6.

Note: Profit will be the balancing figure.

Chapter 2
Ledger accounting

QUESTION 3

Z has the following transactions:

(a)   Pays £4,000 into the bank as capital.
(b)   Buys a computer for £1,000.
(c)   Pays rent of £400.
(d)   Earns £800 for consultancy services.

Write up the ledger accounts for the above.

QUESTION 4

In question 3 above fill in the following table to explain the dual nature of each transaction. The first one is done to explain what to do.

		Debit		Credit	
Transaction		Account	Reason	Account	Reason
(a)	£4,000 capital	Bank	Cash paid into the bank - an asset	Capital	Cash paid in by owner – a liability

QUESTION 5

A makes the following cash transactions:

(a)   Pays £5,000 into the bank as capital.
(b)   Buys goods for £800.
(c)   Pays rent of £500.
(d)   Buys a van for £2,000.
(e)   Sells some of the goods for £600.
(f)   Sells some more of the goods for £700.
(g)   Buys goods for £1,000.
(h)   Buys stationery for £200.
(i)   Takes £500 out of the bank as drawings.

Write up the ledger accounts for the above.

QUESTION 6

B makes the following cash transactions:

(a)   Pays £4,000 into the bank as capital.
(b)   Buys goods for £700.
(c)   Buys champagne to entertain the staff for £300.
(d)   Purchases three computers for £3,000.
(e)   Sells goods for £1,500.
(f)   Draws £500 cash.
(g)   Purchases goods for £1,200.
(h)   Pays telephone bill of £600.
(i)   Receives telephone bill rebate of £200.
(j)   Buys stationery for £157.

Write up the ledger accounts for the above.

QUESTION 7

C makes the following cash transactions:

(a)   Pays £2,000 into the bank as capital.
(b)   Purchases goods for £1,000.
(c)   Buys a van costing £900.
(d)   Sells goods for £2,500.
(e)   Receives £3,000 for consultancy services.
(f)   Purchases goods for £1,000.
(g)   Buys stationery for £260.
(h)   Pays rent of £750.
(i)   Pays staff wages of £600.
(j)   Receives £100 for returned stationery.

Write up the ledger accounts for the above.

QUESTION 8

A sells books to B for £1,000 on credit.
A also sells books to C for £90 credit.
B pays £500 and C pays £90.

Write up these transactions in the ledger accounts of A.

QUESTION 9

X purchases £600 of goods from Y and £750 of goods from Z on credit.

X pays Y £300 and Z £500.

Write up these transactions in the ledger accounts of X.

                                                      KAPLAN PUBLISHING

Chapter 3
Balancing the ledger accounts

QUESTION 10

The following cash book has been written up for the month of May 20X4. There was no opening balance.

Bank

	£		£
Capital	10,000	Computer	1,000
Sales	2,000	Telephone	567
Sales	3,000	Rent	1,500
Sales	2,000	Rates	125
		Stationery	247
		Petrol	49
		Purchases	2,500
		Drawings	500
		Petrol	42

Bring down the balance on the account.

QUESTION 11

The following bank account has been written up during May 20X4. There was no brought forward balance.

Bank

	£		£
Capital	5,000	Purchases	850
Sales	1,000	Fixtures	560
Sales	876	Van	1,500
Rent rebate	560	Rent	1,300
Sales	1,370	Rates	360
		Telephone	220
		Stationery	120
		Petrol	48
		Car repairs	167

Bring down the balance on the account.

QUESTION 12

The following bank account has been written up during June 20X4.

Bank

	£		£
Balance b/f	23,700	Drawings	4,000
Sales	2,300	Rent	570
Sales	1,700	Purchases	6,000
Debtors	4,700	Rates	500
		Salaries	3,600
		Car expenses	460
		Petrol	49
		Petrol	38
		Electricity	210
		Stationery	89

Bring down the balance on the account.

QUESTION 13

X Ltd has analysed its sales in a matrix as follows.

	North	South	East	West	Total
Garden plants	253,865	27,598	315,634	109,521	
Garden equipment	2,734,384	274,393	382,726	3,726,125	
Consultancy	2,438,549	374,385	3,728,398	37,261	
TOTAL					

Cast and cross-cast the matrix.

QUESTION 14

The following is the analysed cash paid book of Y Ltd.

Date	Narrative	Folio	Total	Creditors	Stationery	Rent	Telephone	Postage	Fixed assets	Sundry
				23,894	678	4,563	5,675	456	456	78
				6,743					55,433	467
				56,432	654	675				786
				5,643	564		786	78	564	786
				675	89			675	765	8,943
				6,754	675		785	78	897	98
TOTAL										

Cast and cross-cast the cash book.

Chapter 4
Credit sales – discounts and VAT

QUESTION 15

Calculate the VAT on the following sales:

(a)   A sale for £140.00 plus VAT.
(b)   A sale for £560.00 plus VAT.
(c)   A sale for £780.00 including VAT.
(d)   A sale for £970.00 including VAT.

QUESTION 16

Calculate the VAT on the following sales:

(a)   A sale for £280.00 plus VAT where a settlement discount of 2% is offered.
(b)   A sale for £480.00 plus VAT where a settlement discount of 3% is offered.
(c)   A sale for £800.00 plus VAT where a settlement discount of 5% is offered but not taken.
(d)   A sale of £650.00 plus VAT where a settlement discount of 4% is offered but not taken.

QUESTION 17

A sells £600 of goods to B. VAT has to be added and A offers B a settlement discount of 3%. Calculate the amount that B will pay A if:

(a)   B takes the settlement discount; and
(b)   B does not take the settlement discount.

QUESTION 18

A sells £700 of goods to C net of VAT. A offers C a settlement discount of 5%. Enter the sale and payment for the sale in the ledger accounts assuming:

(a)   C takes the settlement discount; and
(b)   C does not take the settlement discount.

Chapter 5
The sales day book – main and subsidiary ledgers

QUESTION 19

You work in the accounts department of D F Engineering and one of your tasks is to write up the day books. In your organisation there is no separate sales returns day book and therefore any credit notes are entered as negative amounts in the sales day book.

Given below are the details of the sales invoices and credit notes that have been issued this week. D F Engineering does not offer trade or settlement discounts but is registered for VAT and all sales are of standard rated goods.

Invoices sent out:

		Code	£		Invoice number
20X1					
1 May	Fraser & Co	SL14	128.68	plus VAT	03466
	Letterhead Ltd	SL03	257.90	plus VAT	03467
2 May	Jeliteen Traders	SL15	96.58	plus VAT	03468
3 May	Harper Bros	SL22	268.15	plus VAT	03469
	Juniper Ltd	SL17	105.38	plus VAT	03470
4 May	H G Frank	SL30	294.67	plus VAT	03471
5 May	Keller Assocs	SL07	110.58	plus VAT	03472

Credit notes sent out:

		Code	£		Credit note number
20X1					
2 May	Garner & Co	SL12	68.70	plus VAT	0746
4 May	Hill Traders	SL26	117.68	plus VAT	0747

Required

Write up the sales day book given for the week ending 5 May 20X1 and total all of the columns.

Sales day book

Date	Invoice No	Customer name	Code	Total £	VAT £	Net £

QUESTION 20

You work in the accounts department of Keyboard Supplies, a supplier of a wide range of electronic keyboards to a variety of music shops on credit. Given below are three sales invoices that you have just sent out to customers and these are to be written up into the sales day book given below.

Sales of four different types of keyboard are made and the sales are analysed into each of these four types and coded as follows:

Atol keyboards	01
Bento keyboards	02
Garland keyboards	03
Zanni keyboards	04

Required

Write up the analysed sales day book and total each of the columns.

INVOICE

Invoice to:	**Keyboard Supplies**
B Z S Music	Trench Park Estate
42 Westhill	Fieldham
Nutford TN11 3PQ	Sussex TN21 4AF
	Tel: 01829 654545
	Fax: 01829 654646

Deliver to:

As above

Invoice no:	06116
Tax point:	18 April 20X1
VAT reg no:	466 1128 30
Your reference:	SL01
Purchase order no:	77121

Code	Description	Quantity	VAT rate %	Unit price £	Amount exclusive of VAT £
B4012	Bento Keyboard	3	17.5	180.00	540.00
Z2060	Zanni Keyboard	6	17.5	164.00	984.00

	1,524.00
Trade discount 20%	304.80
	1,219.20
VAT at 17.5%	206.95
Total amount payable	1,426.15

Deduct discount of 3% if paid within 10 days, net 30 days

INVOICE

Invoice to:
M T Retail
Fraser House
Perley TN7 8QT

Deliver to:

As above

Keyboard Supplies
Trench Park Estate
Fieldham
Sussex TN21 4AF
Tel: 01829 654545
Fax: 01829 654646

Invoice no: 06117
Tax point: 18 April 20X1
VAT reg no: 466 1128 30
Your reference: SL29
Purchase order no: P04648

Code	Description	Quantity	VAT rate %	Unit price £	Amount exclusive of VAT £
A6060	Atol Keyboard	1	17.5	210.00	210.00
Z4080	Zanni Keyboard	1	17.5	325.00	325.00
					535.00
VAT at 17.5%					93.62
Total amount payable					628.62

Net 30 days

INVOICE

Invoice to:
Harmer & Co
1 Acre Street
Nutford TN11 6HA

Deliver to:

As above

Keyboard Supplies
Trench Park Estate
Fieldham
Sussex TN21 4AF
Tel: 01829 654545
Fax: 01829 654646

Invoice no: 06118
Tax point: 18 April 20X1
VAT reg no: 466 1128 30
Your reference: SL17
Purchase order no: 047721

Code	Description	Quantity	VAT rate %	Unit price £	Amount exclusive of VAT £
G4326	Garland Keyboard	3	17.5	98.00	294.00
B2040	Bento Keyboard	5	17.5	115.00	575.00
					869.00
VAT at 17.5%					147.51
Total amount payable					1,016.51

Deduct discount of 3% if paid within 10 days, net 30 days

Sales day book

Date	Invoice No	Customer name	Code	Total	VAT	01	02	03	04
				£	£	£	£	£	£

QUESTION 21

Graham Haddow runs a buildings maintenance and decorating business and sends out invoices for the work that he has done. He analyses his sales between the maintenance work and decorating work. You are given three sales invoices that he sent out last week.

Required

Enter the sales invoice details into the analysed sales day book given and total all of the columns.

INVOICE

Invoice to:
Portman & Co
Portman House
Tonbridge TN1 4LL

Graham Haddow
59 East Street
Medford
MF6 7TL
Tel: 0122 280496

Invoice no: 07891
Tax point: 1 May 20X1
VAT reg no: 431 7992 06
Your reference: P2

	Amount exclusive of VAT £
Repair of window	66.00
Clearing of guttering	73.00
	139.00
VAT at 17.5%	23.83
Total amount payable	162.83

Deduct discount of 2% if paid within 14 days, net 30 days

INVOICE

Invoice to:
Stanton Associates
323 Main Road
Tonbridge TN1 6EL

Graham Haddow
59 East Street
Medford
MF6 7TL
Tel: 0122 280496
Invoice no: 07892
Tax point: 3 May 20X1
VAT reg no: 431 7992 06
Your reference: S3

	Amount exclusive of VAT £
Decoration of meeting room	1,100.00
VAT at 17.5%	188.65
Total amount payable	1,288.65

Deduct discount of 2% if paid within 14 days, net 30 days

INVOICE

Invoice to:
Boreham Bros
50/54 Hill Drive
Medford MF2 8AT

Graham Haddow
59 East Street
Medford
MF6 7TL
Tel: 0122 280496
Invoice no: 07893
Tax point: 5 May 20X1
VAT reg no: 431 7992 06
Your reference: B7

	Amount exclusive of VAT £
Repair of door frames	106.00
Re-decorating of door frames	130.00
	236.00
VAT at 17.5%	41.30
Total amount payable	277.30

Sales day book

Date	Invoice No	Customer name	Code	Total	VAT	Maintenance	Decorating
				£	£	£	£

QUESTION 22

Given below is an analysed sales day book.

Required

Total the sales day book and check that the totals cross-cast; post the totals to the main ledger accounts; and post the individual entries to the subsidiary ledger accounts.

Sales day book

Date	Invoice No	Customer name	Code	Total	VAT	Group 01	Group 02
				£	£	£	£
20X0							
1 Feb	61612	Worker Ltd	SL11	217.37	32.37	68.90	116.10
4 Feb	61613	P T Associates	SL04	122.38	18.22		104.16
5 Feb	61614	Paul Bros	SL13	289.27	43.08	106.19	140.00
8 Feb	61615	S D Partners	SL07	109.54	16.31	72.40	20.83
9 Feb	61616	Harper Ltd	SL08	399.97	59.57	160.18	180.22
11 Feb	C241	P T Associates	SL04	(23.68)	(3.52)		(20.16)
15 Feb	61617	Worker Ltd	SL11	144.26	21.48	50.60	72.18
17 Feb	61618	P T Associates	SL04	201.67	30.03	60.41	111.23
18 Feb	61619	Harper Ltd	SL08	345.15	51.40	110.15	183.60
22 Feb	C242	Paul Bros	SL13	(35.72)	(5.32)	(10.18)	(20.22)
25 Feb	61620	P T Associates	SL04	129.01	19.21	62.17	47.63
26 Feb	61621	S D Partners	SL07	56.58	8.42	48.16	

QUESTION 23

Given below is an analysed sales returns day book for the month of April.

Required

Post the totals to the main ledger accounts; and post the individual entries to the subsidiary ledger accounts.

Sales returns day book								
Date	Credit note No	Customer name	Code	Total	VAT	01	02	03
				£	£	£	£	£
20X1								
7/4	2114	Gerard & Co	G01	34.36	5.11	16.80		12.45
15/4	2115	Filmer Ltd	F02	44.92	6.69	20.41	17.82	
20/4	2116	T Harrison	H04	24.44	3.64			20.80
28/4	2117	Rolls Ltd	R01	36.47	5.43	16.80	14.24	
				140.19	20.87	54.01	32.06	33.25

Chapter 6
The analysed cash receipts book

QUESTION 24

Your organisation receives a number of cheques from debtors through the post each day and these are listed on the cheque listing. It also makes some cash sales each day which include VAT at the standard rate.

Today's date is 28 April 20X1 and the cash sales today were £265.08. The cheque listing for the day is given below:

Cheque listing 28 April 20X1

G Heilbron	£108.45
L Tessa	£110.57 - settlement discount of £3.31 taken
J Dent	£210.98 - settlement discount of £6.32 taken
F Trainer	£ 97.60
A Winter	£105.60 - settlement discount of £3.16 taken

An extract from the customer file shows the following:

Customer	Sales ledger code
J Dent	SL17
G Heilbron	SL04
L Tessa	SL15
F Trainer	SL21
A Winter	SL09

Required

(a)   Write up the cash receipts book given below; total each of the columns of the cash receipts book and check that they cross-cast

(b)   Post the totals of the cash receipts book to the main ledger accounts.

(c)   Post the individual receipts to the subsidiary ledger, the sales ledger.

Cash receipts book

Date	Narrative	SL Code	Total	VAT	Debtors	Cash sales	Discount
			£	£	£	£	£

QUESTION 25

Given below is the cheque listing for your organisation showing all of the cheques received in the week ending 15 May 20X1.

Customer	Sales ledger code	£	Discount taken £
McCaul & Partners	M04	147.56	2.95
Dunn Associates	D02	264.08	
P Martin	M02	167.45	
F Little	L03	265.89	7.97
D Raine	R01	158.02	3.95

There were also cash sales of £446.50 including standard rate VAT during the week.

Required

(a)   Write up the cash receipts book given for the week; total the columns of the cash receipts book and check that they cross-cast

(b)   Post the totals to the main ledger accounts.

(c)   Post the individual receipts to the subsidiary ledger accounts in the sales ledger.

Cash receipts book

Date	Narrative	SL Code	Total	VAT	Debtors	Cash sales	Discount
			£	£	£	£	£

Chapter 7
Credit purchases – discounts and VAT

QUESTION 26

Calculate the VAT for the following:

(a)   X purchases £400 goods from Y net of VAT.
(b)   X purchases £650 goods from Y net of VAT.
(c)   X purchases £425 goods from Y including VAT.
(d)   X purchases £77 goods from Y including VAT.

QUESTION 27

Calculate the VAT on the following:

(a)   X purchases £850 goods from Y and takes the 3% settlement discount offered.
(b)   X purchases £600 goods from Y and takes the 5% settlement discount offered.
(c)   X purchases £325 goods from Y and does not take the 2% settlement discount offered.
(d)   X purchases £57 goods from Y and does not take the 4% settlement discount offered.

QUESTION 28

Z buys £600 of goods net of VAT from A and takes the 3% settlement discount offered.

Post these transactions in the ledger accounts of Z.

Chapter 8
The purchases day book – main and subsidiary ledgers

QUESTION 29

Curtain Decor is a business that makes curtains and blinds to order. Its purchases are analysed between fabric purchases, header tape purchases and others. A separate purchases returns day book is not kept so any credit notes received are recorded as negative amounts in the purchases day book. The business only has five credit suppliers and they are as follows:

Mainstream Fabrics	PL01
C R Thorne	PL02
Fabric Supplies Ltd	PL03
Lillian Fisher	PL04
Headstream & Co	PL05

Today's date is 12 April 20X1 and given below are three invoices and a credit note. These are to be entered into the analysed purchases day book and each column is to be totalled.

INVOICE

Invoice to:
Curtain Decor
Field House
Warren Lane
Hawkhurst   TN23 1AT

Deliver to:
As above

Fabric Supplies Ltd
12/14 Tike Road
Wadfield
TN11 4ZP
Tel: 01882 467111
Fax: 01882 467112

Invoice no:	06738
Tax point:	7 April 20X1
VAT reg no:	532 6741 09

Code	Description	Quantity	VAT rate %	Unit price £	Amount exclusive of VAT £
B116–14	Header Tape 14 cm	30 m	17.5%	4.62	138.60
P480–G	Fabric - Green	56 m	17.5%	14.25	798.00
					936.60

VAT at 17.5%   160.62

Total amount payable   1,097.22

Deduct discount of 2% if paid within 10 days

INVOICE

LILLIAN FISHER

Invoice to:
Curtain Decor
Field House
Warren Lane
Hawkhurst   TN23 1AT

61 Park Crescent
Hawkhurst
TN23 8GF
Tel: 01868 463501
Fax: 01868 463502

Deliver to:
As above

Invoice no:	0328
Tax point:	6 April 20X1
VAT reg no:	469 7153 20

Code	Description	Quantity	VAT rate %	Unit price £	Amount exclusive of VAT £
TB06	Tie Back Cord - Yellow	10 m	17.5%	6.55	65.50
TB09	Tie Back Cord – Green	4 m	17.5%	6.55	26.20
					91.70
VAT at 17.5%					16.04
Total amount payable					107.74

CREDIT NOTE

Headstream & Co

Credit note to:
Curtain Decor
Field House
Warren Lane
Hawkhurst   TN23 1AT

140 Myrtle Place
Fenham
TN16 4SJ
Tel: 01842 303136
Fax: 01842 303137

Credit note no:	CN0477
Tax point:	7 April 20X1
VAT reg no:	663 4892 77

Code	Description	Quantity	VAT rate %	Unit price £	Amount exclusive of VAT £
HT479	Header Tape 11 cm	2 m	17.5%	8.30	16.60
CCF614Y	CC Fabric - Yellow	4 m	17.5%	12.85	51.40
					68.00
VAT at 17.5%					11.90
Total credit					79.90

INVOICE

Mainstream Fabrics

Tree Tops House
Farm Road
Tonbridge
TN2 4XT
Tel: 01883 214121
Fax: 01883 214122

Invoice no:	07359
Tax point:	8 April 20X1
VAT reg no:	379 4612 04

Code	Description	Quantity	VAT rate %	Unit price £	Amount exclusive of VAT £
DG4167F	Design Guild Fabric - Fuchsia	23 m	17.5%	13.60	312.80

	312.80
Trade discount 10%	31.28
	281.52
VAT at 17.5%	48.52
Total amount payable	330.04

Deduct discount of 1½% if paid within 14 days

Purchases day book

Date	Invoice no	Code	Supplier	Total	VAT	Fabric	Header Tape	Other

QUESTION 30

Nethan Builders analyse their purchases into wood, bricks and cement, and small consumables such as nails and screws. You are given three purchase invoices, recently received, to enter into the purchases day book given.

An extract from the purchase ledger coding manual is given:

Supplier	Purchase ledger code
A J Broom & Co Ltd	PL08
Jenson Ltd	PL13
Magnum Supplies	PL16

Today's date is 3 May 20X1.

Enter the invoices into the analysed purchases day book and total each of the columns.

INVOICE

MAGNUM SUPPLIES

Invoice to:
Nethan Builders
Brecon House
Stamford Road
Manchester
M16 4PL

Deliver to:
As above

140/150 Park Estate
Manchester
M20 6EG
Tel: 0161 561 3202
Fax: 0161 561 3200

Invoice no:	077401
Tax point:	1 May 20X1
VAT reg no:	611 4337 90

Code	Description	Quantity	VAT rate %	Unit price £	Amount exclusive of VAT £
BH47732	House Bricks – Red	400	17.5%	1.24	496.00

	496.00
Trade discount 15%	74.40
	421.60
VAT at 17.5%	72.30
Total amount payable	493.90

Deduct discount of 2% if paid within 10 days

INVOICE

Invoice to:
Nethan Builders
Brecon House
Stamford Road
Manchester
M16 4PL

Deliver to:
As above

A J Broom & Company Limited

59 Parkway
Manchester
M2 6EG
Tel: 0161 560 3392
Fax: 0161 560 5322

Invoice no: 046193
Tax point: 1 May 20X1
VAT reg no: 661 2359 07

Code	Description	Quantity	VAT rate %	Unit price £	Amount exclusive of VAT £
DGT472	SDGS Softwood 47 × 225 mm	11.2 m	17.5%	8.44	94.53
NBD021	Oval Wire Nails 100 mm	7 boxes	17.5%	2.50	17.50

	112.03
Trade discount 10%	11.20
	100.83
VAT at 17.5%	17.64
Total amount payable	118.47

INVOICE

Jenson Ltd

Invoice to:
Nethan Builders
Brecon House
Stamford Road
Manchester
M16 4PL

Deliver to:
As above

30 Longfield Park
Kingsway
M45 2TP
Tel: 0161 511 4666
Fax: 0161 511 4777

Invoice no:	47823
Tax point:	1 May 20X1
VAT reg no:	641 3229 45
Purchase order no:	7211

Code	Description	Quantity	VAT rate %	Unit price £	Amount exclusive of VAT £
PLY8FU	Plywood Hardboard	16 sheets	17.5%	17.80	284.80
BU611	Ventilator Brick	10	17.5%	8.60	86.00
					370.80

VAT at 17.5% 62.94

Total amount payable 433.74

Deduct discount of 3% if paid within 14 days

Purchases day book

Date	Invoice no	Code	Supplier	Total	VAT	Wood	Bricks/ Cement	Consumables

QUESTION 31

Nethan Builders have recently received the three credit notes given. They are to be recorded in the analysed purchases returns day book given.

An extract from the purchase ledger coding manual shows:

Supplier	Purchase ledger code
Jenson Ltd	PL13
Haddow Bros	PL03
Magnum Supplies	PL16

Today's date is 3 May 20X1.

You are required to enter the credit notes into the analysed purchases returns day book and to total each of the columns.

CREDIT NOTE

Jenson Ltd

Credit note to:
Nethan Builders
Brecon House
Stamford Road
Manchester
M16 4PL

30 Longfield Park
Kingsway
M45 2TP
Tel: 0161 511 4666
Fax: 0161 511 4777

Credit note no:	CN06113
Tax point:	28 April 20X1
VAT reg no:	641 3229 45
Sales invoice no:	47792

Code	Description	Quantity	VAT rate %	Unit price £	Amount exclusive of VAT £
PL432115	Door Lining Set – Wood 32 × 115 mm	1	17.5%	30.25	30.25

	30.25
Trade discount 15%	4.54
	25.71
VAT at 17.5%	4.36
Total amount of credit	30.07

CREDIT NOTE

Credit note to:
Nethan Builders
Brecon House
Stamford Road
Manchester
M16 4PL

Haddow Bros

The White House
Standing Way
Manchester
M13 6FH
Tel: 0161 560 3140
Fax: 0161 560 6140

Credit note no: 06132
Tax point: 27 April 20X1
VAT reg no: 460 3559 71

Code	Description	Quantity	VAT rate %	Unit price £	Amount exclusive of VAT £
PLY8FE1	Plywood Hardwood 2440 × 1220 mm	2	17.5%	17.80	35.60
					35.60
VAT at 17.5%					6.10
Total amount of credit					41.70

CREDIT NOTE

Credit note to:
Nethan Builders
Brecon House
Stamford Road
Manchester
M16 4PL

MAGNUM SUPPLIES

140/150 Park Estate
Manchester
M20 6EG
Tel: 0161 561 3202
Fax: 0161 561 3200

Credit note no: C4163
Tax point: 30 April 20X1
VAT reg no: 611 4337 90

Code	Description	Quantity	VAT rate %	Unit price £	Amount exclusive of VAT £
BU1628	Ventilator Brick	5	17.5%	9.20	46.00
					46.00
Trade discount 15%					6.90
					39.10
VAT at 17.5%					6.70
Total amount of credit					45.80

Purchases returns day book								
Date	Credit note no	Code	Supplier	Total	VAT	Wood	Bricks/ Cement	Consumables

QUESTION 32

Given below is a purchases returns day book.

You are required to:

- post the totals to the main ledger accounts;

- post the individual entries to the subsidiary ledger accounts.

Purchases returns day book									
Date	Credit note	Code	Supplier	Total £	VAT £	01 £	02 £	03 £	04 £
15/4/X1	C0179	PL16	J D Withers	27.49	4.09		23.40		
18/4/X1	C4772	PL06	F Williams	164.50	24.50	32.00		108.00	
19/4/X1	06638	PL13	K Bartlett	53.11	7.91	28.40			16.80
				245.10	36.50	60.40	23.40	108.00	16.80

Main ledger

Purchases ledger control account

	£			£
		12/4	Balance b/f	12,678.57

VAT account

	£			£
		12/4	Balance b/f	1,023.90

Purchases returns – 01 account

	£			£
		12/4	Balance b/f	337.60

Purchases returns – 02 account

	£				£
		12/4	Balance b/f		228.59

Purchases returns – 03 account

	£				£
		12/4	Balance b/f		889.46

Purchases returns – 04 account

	£				£
		12/4	Balance b/f		362.78

Subsidiary ledger

F Williams   *PL06*

	£				£
		12/4	Balance b/f		673.47

K Bartlett   *PL13*

	£				£
		12/4	Balance b/f		421.36

J D Withers   *PL16*

	£				£
		12/4	Balance b/f		446.37

QUESTION 33

Given below is the purchases day book for a business.

Purchases day book

Date	Invoice no	Code	Supplier	Total £	VAT £	Net £
20X1						
1 May	36558	PL03	L Jameson	393.91	58.66	335.25
1 May	102785	PL07	K Davison	124.96	18.61	106.35
3 May	92544	PL02	H Samuels	109.79	16.35	93.44
4 May	03542	PL04	G Rails	180.93	26.94	153.99
5 May	002633	PL01	T Ives	192.98	28.74	164.24
				1,002.57	149.30	853.27

You are required to:

- post the totals of the purchases day book to the main ledger accounts given.

- post the individual invoices to the creditors' accounts in the subsidiary ledger given.

Main ledger

Purchases ledger control account

	£			£
		1 May	Balance b/d	3,104.67

VAT account

	£			£
		1 May	Balance b/d	723.56

Purchases account

	£		£
1 May Balance b/d	24,367.48		

Subsidiary ledger

T Ives   PL01

	£			£
		1 May	Balance b/d	332.56

H Samuels   PL02

	£			£
		1 May	Balance b/d	286.90

L Jameson   PL03

	£			£
		1 May	Balance b/d	623.89

G Rails   PL04

	£			£
		1 May	Balance b/d	68.97

K Davison   PL07

	£			£
		1 May	Balance b/d	125.47

Chapter 9
The analysed cash payments book

QUESTION 34

Given below is the cheque listing for a business for the week ending 12 March 20X1.

Cheque payment listing				
Supplier	Code	Cheque number	Cheque amount £	Discount taken £
Homer Ltd	PL12	03648	168.70	5.06
Forker & Co	PL07	03649	179.45	5.38
Cash purchases		03650	334.87	
Print Associates	PL08	03651	190.45	
ABG Ltd	PL02	03652	220.67	6.62
Cash purchases		03653	193.87	
G Greg	PL19	03654	67.89	

You are required to:

- enter the payments into the cash payments book and total each of the columns;
- post the totals to the main ledger accounts given;
- post the individual entries to the subsidiary ledger accounts given.

Cash payments book

Date	Details	Cheque no	Code	Total £	VAT £	Purchases ledger £	Cash purchases £	Other £	Discounts received £

KAPLAN PUBLISHING

Main ledger

Purchases ledger control account

		£				£
			5/3	Balance b/d		4,136.24

VAT account

		£				£
			5/3	Balance b/d		1,372.56

Purchases account

		£				£
5/3	Balance b/d	20,465.88				

Discounts received account

		£				£
			5/3	Balance b/d		784.56

Subsidiary ledger

ABG Ltd   PL02

		£				£
			5/3	Balance b/d		486.90

Forker & Co   PL07

		£				£
			5/3	Balance b/d		503.78

Print Associates   PL08

		£				£
			5/3	Balance b/d		229.56

Homer Ltd   PL12

		£				£
			5/3	Balance b/d		734.90

G Greg   PL19

		£				£
			5/3	Balance b/d		67.89

QUESTION 35

Given below is the cheque listing for Nethan Builders for the week ended 30 May 20X1.

Cheque listing

Supplier	Code	Cheque number	Cheque amount £	Discount taken £
J M Bond	PL01	200572	247.56	
Magnum Supplies	PL16	200573	662.36	13.25
A J Broom Ltd	PL08	200574	153.57	
Jenson Ltd	PL13	200575	336.57	6.73
KKL Traders	PL20	200576	442.78	8.85
Cash purchases		200577	108.66	

The figure for cash purchases includes VAT at 17.5%.

You are required to:

- enter these amounts in the cash payments book provided and to total each of the columns;

- post the totals to the main ledger accounts given;

- post the individual entries to the subsidiary ledger accounts given.

Cash payments book

Date	Details	Cheque no	Code	Total £	VAT £	Purchases ledger £	Cash purchases £	Other £	Discounts received £

Main ledger

Purchases ledger control account

	£			£
		23 May	Balance b/d	5,328.46

VAT account

	£			£
		23 May	Balance b/d	1,365.35

Purchases account

		£		£
23 May	Balance b/d	36,785.90		

Discount received account

	£			£
		23 May	Balance b/d	1,573.56

Subsidiary ledger

J M Bond   PL01

	£			£
		23 May	Balance b/d	247.56

A J Broom Ltd   PL08

	£			£
		23 May	Balance b/d	524.36

Jenson Ltd   PL13

	£			£
		23 May	Balance b/d	512.36

Magnum Supplies   PL16

	£			£
		23 May	Balance b/d	675.61

KKL Traders   PL20

	£			£
		23 May	Balance b/d	612.46

Chapter 10
Credit sales: documents

QUESTION 36

You have been given details of goods that have been returned to Keyboard Supplies. The return has been checked and authorised and you are now to prepare the credit note.

Return from: H H Music   SL 09
                  Tenant House   Trade discount 15%
                  Perley
                  TN7 8ER

Goods returned: 1 Bento keyboard   Code B3060   Unit price (before VAT and discount) £126.00

Reason for return: Goods not ordered

Today's date is 17 April 20X1 and the last credit note to have been issued was CN 0336.

Required

Prepare the credit note on the blank credit note given below.

CREDIT NOTE

Credit Note to:

Keyboard Supplies
Trench Park Estate
Fieldham
Sussex TN21 4AF
Tel: 01829 654545
Fax: 01829 654646

Credit Note no:
Tax point:
VAT reg no: 466 1128 30
Your reference:
Purchase order no:

Code	Description	Quantity	VAT rate %	Unit price £	Amount exclusive of VAT £

Trade discount   %

VAT at 17.5%

Total amount

QUESTION 37

You work in the accounts department of Keyboard Supplies, a supplier of a wide range of electronic keyboards to a variety of music shops on credit. Given below are three purchase orders for goods which are due to be despatched today.

You also have an extract from the customer master file:

Customer	Sales ledger code	Trade discount	Settlement discount
F T Music Supplies	SL23	15%	–
Musicolor Ltd	SL06	10%	3% – 10 days
Newford Music	SL18	20%	3% – 10 days

Today's date is 17 April 20X1 and the last sales invoice to be sent out was invoice number 06112. Normal credit terms are 30 days although some customers are offered a settlement discount. The business is registered for VAT and all of the goods are standard rated.

Required

Complete the sales invoices for these sales on the blank invoices supplied.

PURCHASE ORDER

Musicolor Ltd
23 High Street
Nutford
Sussex TN11 4TZ
Tel: 01826 434111
Fax: 01826 434112
Date: 12 April 20X1
Purchase order no: 04318

To: Keyboard Supplies
             Trench Park Estate
             Fieldham
             Sussex TN21 4AF

Delivery address
(If different from above)

Invoice address
(If different from above)

Code	Quantity	Description	Unit price (exclusive of VAT and discounts) £
Z4600	2	Zanni Keyboard	185.00
A4802	3	Atol Keyboard	130.00

PURCHASE ORDER

Newford Music
32/34 Main Street
Welland
Sussex TN4 6BD
Tel: 01760 437711
Fax: 01760 436204
Date: 10 April 20X1
Purchase order no: 47115

To: Keyboard Supplies
Trench Park Estate
Fieldham
Sussex TN21 4AF

Delivery address (If different from above)	**Invoice address** (If different from above)

Code	Quantity	Description	Unit price (exclusive of VAT and discounts) £
Z4406	4	Zanni Keyboard	165.00

PURCHASE ORDER

F T Music Supplies
The Barn
Nutford
Sussex TN11 7AJ
Tel: 01826 431799
Fax: 01826 431800
Date: 13 April 20X1
Purchase order no: 71143

To: Keyboard Supplies
Trench Park Estate
Fieldham
Sussex TN21 4AF

Delivery address (If different from above)	**Invoice address** (If different from above)

Code	Quantity	Description	Unit price (exclusive of VAT and discounts) £
B2010	2	Bento Keyboard	148.00
G4706	3	Garland Keyboard	96.00

INVOICE

Invoice to:

Deliver to:

Keyboard Supplies
Trench Park Estate
Fieldham
Sussex TN21 4AF
Tel: 01829 654545
Fax: 01829 654646

Invoice no:
Tax point:
VAT reg no: 466 1128 30
Your reference:
Purchase order no:

Code	Description	Quantity	VAT rate %	Unit price £	Amount exclusive of VAT £

Trade discount   %

VAT at 17.5%
Total amount payable

INVOICE

Invoice to:

Deliver to:

Keyboard Supplies
Trench Park Estate
Fieldham
Sussex TN21 4AF
Tel: 01829 654545
Fax: 01829 654646

Invoice no:
Tax point:
VAT reg no: 466 1128 30
Your reference:
Purchase order no:

Code	Description	Quantity	VAT rate %	Unit price £	Amount exclusive of VAT £

Trade discount   %
VAT at 17.5%
Total amount payable

INVOICE

Keyboard Supplies
Trench Park Estate
Fieldham
Sussex TN21 4AF
Tel: 01829 654545
Fax: 01829 654646

Invoice to:

Deliver to:

Invoice no:
Tax point:
VAT reg no: 466 1128 30
Your reference:
Purchase order no:

Code	Description	Quantity	VAT rate %	Unit price £	Amount exclusive of VAT £

Trade discount   %

VAT at 17.5%
Total amount payable

Chapter 11
Debtors' statements

QUESTION 38

You work in the accounts department of Farmhouse Pickles Ltd and given below are two debtors' accounts from the subsidiary sales ledger.

Grant & Co   SL07

		£			£
1 April	Balance b/d	337.69	12 April	SRDB – 0335	38.70
4 April	SDB 32656	150.58	20 April	CRB	330.94
18 April	SDB 32671	179.52	20 April	CRB – discount	6.75
25 April	SDB 32689	94.36	24 April	SRDB – 0346	17.65

Mitchell Partners   SL10

		£			£
1 April	Balance b/d	180.46	12 April	SRDB – 0344	66.89
7 April	SDB 32662	441.57	21 April	CRB	613.58
20 April	SDB 32669	274.57	21 April	CRB – discount	8.45

Required

Prepare statements to be sent to each of these customers at the end of April 20X1 on the blank statements provided.

FARMHOUSE PICKLES LTD

225 School Lane
Weymouth
Dorset
WE36 5NR

Tel: 0261 480444
Fax: 0261 480555
Date:

To:

STATEMENT

Date	Transaction	Debit £	Credit £	Balance £

May we remind you that our credit terms are 30 days

| | | FARMHOUSE PICKLES LTD | | |

		225 School Lane
		Weymouth
To:		Dorset
		WE36 5NR
		Tel: 0261 480444
		Fax: 0261 480555
		Date:

STATEMENT

Date	Transaction	Debit £	Credit £	Balance £

May we remind you that our credit terms are 30 days

QUESTION 39

Today is 4 December 20X1. You are the sales ledger clerk at Toybox Games Ltd, a manufacturer of board games supplied to the toy market.

Cash received during the previous week has already been posted to the main ledger and the subsidiary (sales) ledger.

You have just received the sales day book from the accounts assistant, Andrew Donnelly. He has already prepared a journal entry.

Task 1   Check the journal entry form and correct it if necessary.

Task 2   Post the totals for the week ending 30 November 20X1 to the correct main ledger accounts.

Task 3   Post the individual transactions to the correct debtors accounts in the subsidiary (sales) ledger.

Task 4   You now turn your attention to the sales returns day book. Total the sales returns day book.

Task 5   Prepare the journal entry required to post the sales returns day book.

Task 6   Post the totals of the sales returns day book to the correct main ledger accounts.

Task 7 Post the individual transactions from the sales returns day book to the correct debtors accounts in the subsidiary (sales) ledger.

Task 8 Prepare statements to send to Daisychains and Jubilee Games & Toys.

Sales Day Book

Date	Code	Customer	Invoice	Total £		01 £		02 £		03 £		04 £		VAT £	
26/11/X1	D2	Daisychains	2205	1,661	63	205	25					1,208	90	247	48
	J2	Jubilee Games	2206	4,325	30			3,681	11					644	19
27/11/X1	M3	Mirabelle Leisure	2207	954	04							811	95	142	09
	A2	Arnold Toys	2208	456	19	388	25							67	94
	H3	Highlight Ltd	2209	260	98					222	11			38	87
28/11/X1	L1	Lighthouse Products	2210	7,069	34			2,065	18	3,951	28			1,052	88
	D2	Daisychains	2211	2,057	17	580	33			459	27	711	18	306	39
29/11/X1	G4	Gameboard Ltd	2212	2,657	24			1,538	98	722	50			395	76
	M3	Mirabelle Leisure	2213	946	82	221	95	381	55	202	30			141	02
30/11/X1	B2	Gerald Blythe	2214	629	68							535	90	93	78
		Total		21,018	39	1,395	78	7,666	82	5,557	46	3,267	93	3,130	40

Sales returns day book

Date	Code	Customer	CN	Total £	01 £	02 £	03 £	04 £	VAT £
26/11/X1	B2	Gerald Blythe	C461	190.11				161.80	28.31
30/11/X1	H3	Highlight Ltd	C462	47.70			40.60		7.10
30/11/X1	L1	Lighthouse Products	C463	228.37		111.16	83.20		34.01

SUBSIDIARY (SALES) LEDGER ACCOUNTS

Customer name   Arnold Toys   Account number   A2
Customer address   57 Gray Street Bath BA1 2NT
Telephone   01225 633112
Dr   Cr

Date	Transaction	£		Date	Transaction	£	
19/11	Invoice 2195	118	08	20/11	CR 2198	323	60
20/11	Invoice 2198	2,201	95		c/f	1,996	43
		2,320	03			2,320	03
23/11	b/f	1,996	43	27/11	Cash	118	08
				29/11	Cash	118	08

Customer name   Gerald Blythe & Sons   Account number   B2
Customer address   121 St John's Road Cambridge CB2 3AH
Telephone   01223 461922
Dr   Cr

Date	Transaction	£		Date	Transaction	£	
12/11	Invoice 2186	325	11	20/11	Cash	325	11
22/11	Invoice 2203	119	80		c/f	119	80
		444	91			444	91
23/11	b/f	119	80				

KAPLAN PUBLISHING

SUBSIDIARY (SALES) LEDGER ACCOUNTS

Customer name   Daisychains   Account number   D2
Customer address   111 George Street Crawley RH10 1HL
Telephone   01293 811566
Dr   Cr

Date	Transaction	£		Date	Transaction	£	
13/9	Invoice 2103	3,115	11 ✓				
27/9	Invoice 2122	211	55		c/f	3,326	66
		3,326	66			3,326	66
28/9	b/f	3,326	66	19/10	Cash	3,115	11 ✓
16/10	Invoice 2150	501	30		c/f	712	85
		3,827	96			3,827	96
19/10	b/f	712	85				
23/10	Invoice 2157	871	07		c/f	1,583	92
		1,583	92			1,583	92
26/10	b/f	1,583	92				

Customer name   Gameboard Ltd   Account number   G4
Customer address   15 Park Street Woking GU21 1BY
Telephone   01483 757442
Dr   Cr

Date	Transaction	£		Date	Transaction	£	
2/11	b/f	3	09	8/11	Cr	3	09
14/11	Invoice 2187	115	83	16/11	CONTRA	86	94
					c/f	28	89
		115	83			115	83
16/11	b/f	28	89	20/11	Cash	28	89

SUBSIDIARY (SALES) LEDGER ACCOUNTS

Customer name   Highlight Ltd   Account number   H3
Customer address   10 Station Road St Albans AL4 3EH
Telephone   01727 46737
Dr   Cr

Date	Transaction	£		Date	Transaction	£	
2/11	Invoice 2173	202	95✓	14/9	b/f	33	75✓
					c/f	169	20
		202	95			202	95
2/11	b/f	169	20	16/11	Cash	169	20✓
14/11	Invoice 2185	311	87✓		c/f	311	87
		481	07			481	07
16/11	b/f	311	87	22/11	Cash	311	87✓

Customer name   Jubilee Games & Toys   Account number   J2
Customer address   3 Bourne Avenue Bracknell RG12 1AR
Telephone   01344 678222
Dr   Cr

Date	Transaction	£		Date	Transaction	£	
23/10	Invoice 2159	86	90	13/11	Cash	73	20

SUBSIDIARY (SALES) LEDGER ACCOUNTS

Customer name	Lighthouse Products		Account number		L1	
Customer address	135 Chapel Road Windsor S14 1UL					
Telephone	01753 828688					
Dr						Cr

Date	Transaction	£		Date	Transaction	£	
13/11	Invoice 2188	326	11	20/11	CONTRA	44	22
	c/f	44	22	21/11	Cash	326	11
		370	33			370	33
				23/11	b/f	44	22

Customer name	Mirabelle Leisure		Account number		M3	
Customer address	19 Masons Hill Brighton BN1 8RT					
Telephone	01273 207146					
Dr						Cr

Date	Transaction	£		Date	Transaction	£	
14/11	Invoice 2189	411	38				
15/11	Invoice 2190	83	91		c/f	495	29
		495	29			495	29
16/11	b/f	495	29	20/11	Cash	459	29
					c/f	36	00
		495	29			495	29
23/11	b/f	36	00				

MAIN LEDGER

Account name Sales ledger control   Account no   01 06 10 00

23/11/X1	b/f	3,705.63	27/11/X1	Cash	118.08
			29/11/X1	Cash	118.08

Account name Sales - Product 01   Account no   03 70 10 01

		23/11/X1 b/f	34,875.94

Account name Sales - Product 02   Account no   03 70 10 02

		23/11/X1 b/f	175,311.50

Account name Sales - Product 03   Account no   03 70 10 03

		23/11/X1 b/f	123,844.73

Account name Sales - Product 04   Account no   03 70 10 04

		23/11/X1 b/f	78,914.90

KAPLAN PUBLISHING

Account name   VAT control   Account no   02 08 90 00

	23/11/X1 b/f 20,935.86

Account name   Sales returns – Product 01   Account no   04 60 10 01

23/11/X1 b/f 3,105.89	

Account name   Sales returns – Product 02   Account no   04 60 10 02

23/11/X1 b/f 15,222.75	

Account name   Sales returns – Product 03   Account no   04 60 10 03

23/11/X1 b/f 10,413.67	

Account name   Sales returns – Product 04   Account no   04 60 10 04

23/11/X1 b/f 6,116.70	

JOURNAL	SALES DAY BOOK POSTINGS		NO 3347
Prepared by	A Donnelly	Week ending	30/11/X1
Authorised by			

Account	Debit	Credit
Sales ledger control	21,018.39	
Sales product 01		1,395.78
Sales product 02		7,666.82
Sales product 03		5,557.46
Sales product 04		3,267.93
VAT		3,130.40
TOTALS	21,018.39	21,018.39

JOURNAL	SALES RETURNS DAY BOOK POSTINGS		NO 3348
Prepared by		Week ending	30/11/X1
Authorised by			

Account	Debit	Credit
VAT		
TOTALS		

KAPLAN PUBLISHING

TOYBOX GAMES LTD

125 Finchley Way Bristol BS1 4PL Tel: 01272 200299

STATEMENT OF ACCOUNT

Customer name

Customer account no

Customer address

Statement date		Dr		Cr		Balance	
Date	Transaction	£	p	£	p	£	p

TOYBOX GAMES LTD

125 Finchley Way Bristol BS1 4PL Tel: 01272 200299

STATEMENT OF ACCOUNT

Customer name

Customer account no

Customer address

Statement date		Dr		Cr		Balance	
Date	Transaction	£	p	£	p	£	p

Chapter 12
Accounting for sales – summary

QUESTION 40

Today is 16 May 20X0. You are a ledger clerk in Elliott Brook Associates, a business providing temporary catering staff to hotels on the south coast of England. You have been sent the memorandum reproduced below, from Andrew Brook, the chief accountant.

Task 1   Check the following batch of invoices prepared by the sales ledger clerk as clerically accurate. Show any corrections needed on the face of the invoice.

Task 2   Enter the (corrected) invoices in the sales day book provided.

Task 3   Check the following batch of credit notes prepared by the sales ledger clerk for authorisation, and note any errors.

Task 4   Enter the (corrected) credit notes in the credit notes day book provided. (This is the same as a sales returns day book but 'returns' are not relevant to a service industry.)

MEMORANDUM

To:	A Student	cc:	A N Other
From:	Andrew Brook		
Subject:	Rates and discounts	Date:	20 March 20X0

Please note the following new rates and discounts (with effect from 25 March 20X0).

Grade	Rate per hour £
A	7.50 plus VAT
B	6.25 plus VAT
C	4.00 plus VAT
D	3.00 plus VAT

Invoice equal to or over £	Discount %
300.00	10
500.00	20

Please also note that no credit notes should be issued unless I have authorised them in writing on the face of the credit note.

SALES INVOICE

ELLIOTT BROOK ASSOCIATES

39114

Address
25 Eaton Terrace
Eastbourne BN16 3RS
VAT Reg No   544 2900 17

Telephone 01323 866755
Fax 01323 995655
Tax point **16 May 20X0**

Hire of staff

FAO Catering Manager
Imperial Hotel
45 The Promenade
Eastbourne

Client code IMP 23

Name	Start	Finish	Hours	Grade	Rate £	Total excl VAT £
Wilson	7/5/X0	13/5/X0	40	A	7.50	300.00
			Discount			30.00
						270.00
			VAT at 17.5%			47.25
						317.25 : £317.25

SALES INVOICE

ELLIOTT BROOK ASSOCIATES

39115

Address
25 Eaton Terrace
Eastbourne BN16 3RS
VAT Reg No   544 2900 17

Telephone 01323 866755
Fax 01323 995655
Tax point **16 May 20X0**

Hire of staff

FAO Catering Manager
Rosetree Hotel
355 The Promenade
Eastbourne

Client code ROS 10

Name	Start	Finish	Hours	Grade	Rate £	Total excl VAT £
Stewart	11/5/X0	15/5/X0	11	B	6.25	68.75
Brightwell	7/5/X0	14/5/X0	32	C	4.00	128.00
						196.75
			Discount			0
						196.75
			VAT at 17.5%			34.43
						231.18 : £231.18

SALES INVOICE

ELLIOTT BROOK ASSOCIATES

39116

Address
25 Eaton Terrace
Eastbourne BN16 3RS
VAT Reg No   544 2900 17

Telephone   01323 866755
Fax   01323 995655
Tax point   **16 May 20X0**

Hire of staff

FAO The Manager
West Bay Hotel
67 Western Drive
Eastbourne

Client code WST 02

Name	Start	Finish	Hours	Grade	Rate £	Total excl VAT £
Brown	15/5/X0	15/5/X0	5	B	6.25	31.25
Robinson	8/5/X0	13/5/X0	37	C	4.00	148.00
						179.25
			Discount			0
						179.25
			VAT at 17.5%			31.37
						210.62 : £210.62

SALES INVOICE

ELLIOTT BROOK ASSOCIATES

39118

Address
25 Eaton Terrace
Eastbourne BN16 3RS
VAT Reg No   544 2900 17

Telephone   01323 866755
Fax   01323 995655
Tax point   **16 May 20X0**

Hire of staff

FAO The Manager
Kenmare Hotel
73 East Sands Way
Eastbourne

Client code KEN 11

Name	Start	Finish	Hours	Grade	Rate £	Total excl VAT £
Price	10/5/X0	13/5/X0	12	D	3.00	36.00
Haines	11/5/X0	13/5/X0	16	C	4.00	64.00
Peters	7/5/X0	12/5/X0	30	B	6.25	97.50
						197.50
			Discount			0
						197.50
			VAT at 17.5%			34.56
						232.06 : £232.06

KAPLAN PUBLISHING

SALES INVOICE

ELLIOTT BROOK ASSOCIATES

39119

Address
25 Eaton Terrace
Eastbourne BN16 3RS
VAT Reg No **544 2900 17**

Telephone   01323 866755
Fax   01323 995655
Tax point   **16 May 20X0**

Hire of staff
FAO Trina Watts
Seaview Hotel
173 East Sands Way
Eastbourne
Client code SEA 05

Name	Start	Finish	Hours	Grade	Rate £	Total excl VAT £
Clark	9/5/X0	13/5/X0	16	A	7.50	120.00
Frost	10/5/X0	13/5/X0	20	D	3.00	60.00
						180.00
			Discount			0
						180.00
			VAT at 17.5%			31.50
						211.50 : £211.50

SALES INVOICE

ELLIOTT BROOK ASSOCIATES

39120

Address
25 Eaton Terrace
Eastbourne BN16 3RS
VAT Reg No   **544 2900 17**

Telephone   01323 866755
Fax   01323 995655
Tax point   **16 May 20X0**

Hire of staff
FAO Services Manager
Royal Hotel
Royal View
Eastbourne
Client code ROY 05

Name	Start	Finish	Hours	Grade	Rate £	Total excl VAT £
Clarke	7/5/X0	8/5/X0	15	A	7.50	112.50
Hartley	9/5/X0	13/5/X0	40	A	7.50	300.00
						412.50
			Discount			0
						412.50
			VAT at 17.5%			72.19
						484.69 : £484.69

SALES INVOICE

ELLIOTT BROOK ASSOCIATES

39121

Address
25 Eaton Terrace
Eastbourne BN16 3RS
VAT Reg No   **544 2900 17**

Telephone   01323 866755
Fax   01323 995655
Tax point   **16 May 20X0**

Hire of staff
FAO Sheila Green
Crown and Anchor
Royal View
Eastbourne

Client code CRO 12

Name	Start	Finish	Hours	Grade	Rate £	Total excl VAT £
Chadwick	11/5/X0	13/5/X0	10	D	3.00	30.00
						30.00
		Discount				0
						30.00
		VAT at 17.5%				5.25
						35.25 : £35.35

CREDIT NOTE

ELLIOTT BROOK ASSOCIATES

12233

Address
25 Eaton Terrace
Eastbourne BN16 3RS
VAT Reg No   **544 2900 17**

Telephone   01323 866755
Fax   01323 995655
Tax point   **16 May 20X0**

Reason for credit Clerical error on invoice 38999

FAO Services Manager
Royal Hotel
Royal View
Eastbourne

Client code ROY 05

Name	Start	Finish	Hours	Grade	Adjustment excl VAT £
Clarke					12.90
	VAT at 17.5%				2.26
					15.16

A Brook

CREDIT NOTE

ELLIOTT BROOK ASSOCIATES

12235

Address
25 Eaton Terrace
Eastbourne BN16 3RS
VAT Reg No   **544 2900 17**

Telephone   01323 866755
Fax   01323 995655
Tax point   **16 May 20X0**

Reason for credit Clerical error on invoice 38999

FAO Services Manager
Royal Hotel
Royal View
Eastbourne

Client code ROY 05

Name	Start	Finish	Hours	Grade	Adjustment excl VAT £
Clarke					12.90
			VAT at 17.5%		2.26
					15.16

CREDIT NOTE

ELLIOTT BROOK ASSOCIATES

12236

Address
25 Eaton Terrace
Eastbourne BN16 3RS
VAT Reg No   **544 2900 17**

Telephone   01323 866755
Fax   01323 995655
Tax point   **16 May 20X0**

Reason for credit Discount omitted from invoice 39101

FAO Services Manager
Sandringham Hotel
101 The Promenade
Eastbourne

Client code SAN 10

Name	Start	Finish	Hours	Grade	Adjustment excl VAT £
					45.89
			A Brook		
			VAT at 17.5%		8.03
					53.92

SALES DAY BOOK

DATE	CLIENT	INVOICE	NET	VAT	GROSS

CREDIT NOTES DAY BOOK

DATE	CLIENT	CREDIT NO	NET	VAT	GROSS

KAPLAN PUBLISHING

QUESTION 41

Given below is a completed sales day book for the week ending 26 April 20X1.

Required

Post the totals of the sales day book to the main ledger accounts; and post each individual invoice to the subsidiary ledger (sales ledger) accounts.

Sales day book						
Date	Invoice No	Customer name	Code	Total	VAT	Net
				£	£	£
20X1						
22 April	4671	J T Howard	SL15	138.93	20.69	118.24
22 April	4672	F Parker	SL07	99.07	14.75	84.32
23 April	4673	Harlow Ltd	SL02	125.10	18.63	106.47
24 April	4674	Edmunds & Co	SL13	167.75	24.98	142.77
26 April	4675	Peters & Co	SL09	113.04	16.83	96.21
				643.89	95.88	548.01

QUESTION 42

Given below is an analysed sales day book.

Required

Total the sales day book and check that the totals cross-cast; post the totals to the main ledger accounts; and post the individual entries to the subsidiary ledger accounts.

Sales day book								
Date	Invoice No	Customer name	Code	Total	VAT	01	02	03
				£	£	£	£	£
20X0								
6/9	04771	Harold Ellis	H03	93.77	13.96	15.68		64.13
7/9	04772	P Pilot	P01	134.67	20.05		114.62	
	04773	R Tracy	T02	83.30	12.40	23.22	30.80	16.88
8/9	C0612	Harold Ellis	H03	(15.51)	(2.31)			(13.20)
9/9	04774	Planet Inc	P04	165.34	24.62		64.82	75.90
10/9	04775	Harold Ellis	H03	47.23	7.03	23.80	16.40	
	C0613	C Calver	C01	(17.17)	(2.55)	(8.20)		(6.42)

QUESTION 43

Today is 19 February 20X0. You are the cashier at Paperbox Ltd.

You are required to complete the following tasks.

Task 1	Using the remittance lists prepare the paying in slip and credit card voucher summary for paying these amounts in to the bank.
Task 2	Write up the cash book for monies included on the paying in slip.
	Mail order sales are recorded on the remittance list including VAT.
Task 3	Prepare a journal entry to post the **totals** from the cash receipts book to the accounts in the main ledger.

The last journal entry was number 105.

REMITTANCE LIST

Date   19 - 2 - X0

Receipts from   *TRADE DEBTORS*

Customer name	Invoice No	Cheque £	Credit Card Express £	Credit Card Global £	Discount £
NJ Peal	5229, 5248	291.60			
Stationery Supplies	5392	245.30			5.01
Candle Company Ltd	5227, 5309	562.80			4.95
Pearce & Fellows	5308	659.18			13.45
Abraham Matthews Ltd	5291	117.93			
Total		1,876.81			23.41

REMITTANCE LIST

Date   *19 - 2 - X0*

Receipts from   *Mail Order*

Customer name	Invoice No	Cheque £	Credit Card Express £	Credit Card Global £	Discount £
KB Smith			22.60		
R Jones			5.83		
C Bastok			26.18		
J Rirolli			18.95		
Total			73.56		

KAPLAN PUBLISHING

REMITTANCE LIST

Date: 19 - 2 - X0

Receipts from: *Sundry*

Customer name	Invoice No	Cheque £	Credit Card Express £	Credit Card Global £	Discount £
RF Wholesalers Ltd	*Rent*	*539.50*			
(Not trade debtor)					
(Exempt from VAT)					
Total		539.50			

Bank paying-in slip

		£	brought forward	£	brought forward	£

To be retained by receiving bank

For the credit of _____

Cheques etc for collection to be included in total credit of £ _____ paid in_____ 20__.

	£	brought forward	£	brought forward	£
Carried forward £		carried forward	£	Total cheques etc	£

Date _____

Cashier's stamp and initials

56 – 28 – 48

FINANCIAL BANK PLC

GREENOCK

£50 Notes		
£20 Notes		
£10 Notes		
£5 Notes		
£2 Coins		
£1 Coins		
50p		
20p		
Silver		
Bronze		
Total Cash		
Cheques, POs etc		
TOTAL £		

Fee	No Chqs

Paid in by _____

Address/Ref No. _____

Credit card voucher summary

Please do not pin or staple
this voucher as this will affect
the machine processing.

All sales vouchers must be
deposited within three banking
days of the dates shown on them.

If you are submitting more than 26
vouchers please enclose a separate listing.

If a voucher contravenes the terms of
the retailer agreement then the amount
shown on the voucher may be charged
back to your bank account, either
direct or via your paying in branch.

Similarly, if the total amount shown
on the Retail Voucher Summary does
not balance with our total of vouchers, the
difference will be credited (or debited)
to your bank account.

	£	p
1		
2		
3		
4		
5		
6		
7		
8		
9		
10		
11		
12		
13		
14		
15		
16		
17		
18		
19		
20		
21		
22		
23		
24		
25		
26		

SALES VOUCHERS   TOTAL

	£	p
1		
2		
3		
4		
5		
6		
7		

REFUND VOUCHERS   TOTAL

Cash Book Receipts

Date	Narrative	Paying-in slip no	Total	Debtors	Mail Order Sales	Other	VAT	Discount allowed

Journal no. _____

Date _____

Prepared by _____

Code	Account	Debit		Credit	
506	Cash at bank (deposit)				
601	Bank overdraft				
102	Sales mail order				
202	Bank interest				
504	Trade debtors				
605	VAT control account				
409	Discounts allowed				
504	Trade debtors				
Total					
Narrative					

Chapter 13
Credit purchases: documents

QUESTION 44

Nethan Builders have just received the following credit note. You are required to check that the credit note is clerically accurate and note the details of any problems.

CREDIT NOTE

J M Bond & Co

Credit note to:
Nethan Builders
Brecon House
Stamford Road
Manchester
M16 4PL

North Park Industrial Estate
Manchester
M12 4TU
Tel: 0161 561 3214
Fax: 0161 561 3060

Credit note no:	06192
Tax point:	22 April 20X1
VAT reg no:	461 4367 91
Invoice no:	331624

Code	Description	Quantity	VAT rate %	Unit price £	Amount exclusive of VAT £
DGSS4163	Structural Softwood Untreated	6 m	17.5%	6.85	41.10

	41.10
Trade discount 15%	8.22
	32.88
VAT at 17.5%	5.75
Total amount of credit	38.63

QUESTION 45

You work in the accounts department of Nethan Builders and given below are three purchase invoices together with the related purchase orders and delivery note. You are to check each invoice carefully and note any problems or discrepancies that you find.

INVOICE

A J Broom & Company Limited

Invoice to:
Nethan Builders
Brecon House
Stamford Road
Manchester
M16 4PL

59 Parkway
Manchester
M2 6EG
Tel: 0161 560 3392
Fax: 0161 560 5322

Deliver to:
As above

Invoice no:	046123
Tax point:	22 April 20X1
VAT reg no:	661 2359 07
Purchase order no:	7164

Code	Description	Quantity	VAT rate %	Unit price £	Amount exclusive of VAT £
DGS472	SDG Softwood	9.6 m	17.5%	8.44	81.02
CIBF653	Joist hanger	7	17.5%	12.30	86.10

	167.12
Trade discount 10%	16.71
	150.41
VAT at 17.5%	26.32
Total amount payable	176.73

INVOICE

Invoice to:
Nethan Builders
Brecon House
Stamford Road
Manchester
M16 4PL

Deliver to:
As above

Jenson Ltd

30 Longfield Park
Kingsway
M45 2TP
Tel: 0161 511 4666
Fax: 0161 511 4777

Invoice no: 47792
Tax point: 22 April 20X1
VAT reg no: 641 3229 45
Purchase order no: 7162

Code	Description	Quantity	VAT rate %	Unit price £	Amount exclusive of VAT £
PL432115	Door lining set 32 × 115 mm	14	17.5%	30.25	423.50
PL432140	Door lining set 32 × 138 mm	8	17.5%	33.15	265.20
					688.70
Trade discount 15%					103.30
					585.40
VAT at 17.5%					102.44
Total amount payable					687.84

Deduct discount of 3% if paid within 14 days.

INVOICE

Haddow Bros

Invoice to:
Nethan Builders
Brecon House
Stamford Road
Manchester
M16 4PL

The White House
Standing Way
Manchester
M13 6FH
Tel: 0161 560 3140
Fax: 0161 560 6140

Deliver to:
As above

Invoice no:	033912
Tax point:	22 April 20X1
VAT reg no:	460 3559 71

Code	Description	Quantity	VAT rate %	Unit price £	Amount exclusive of VAT £
PLY8FE1	Plywood Hardwood 2440 × 1220 mm	12 sheets	17.5%	17.80	213.60
					213.60

VAT at 17.5%

					36.63

Total amount payable

					250.23

Deduct discount of 2% if paid within 10 days.

PURCHASE ORDER

Nethan Builders

Brecon House
Stamford Road
Manchester
M16 4PL
Tel: 0161 521 6411
Fax: 0161 521 6412
Date: 14 April 20X1
Purchase order no: 7162

To: Jenson Ltd
30 Longfield Park
Kingsway
M45 2TP

Delivery address
(If different from above)

-

Invoice address
(If different from above)

-

Code	Quantity	Description		Unit price (exclusive of VAT) £
PL432140	8	Door lining set	32 × 138 mm	33.15
PL432115	14	Door lining set	32 × 115 mm	30.25

Nethan Builders

Brecon House
Stamford Road
Manchester
M16 4PL
Tel: 0161 521 6411
Fax: 0161 521 6412
Date: 14 April 20X1
Purchase order no: 7164

To: A J Broom & Co Ltd
59 Parkway
Manchester
M2 6EG

Delivery address
(If different from above)

-

Invoice address
(If different from above)

-

Code	Quantity	Description	Unit price (exclusive of VAT) £
DGS472	9.6 m	SDG Softwood	8.44
CIBF653	5	Joist hanger	12.30

PURCHASE ORDER

Nethan Builders

Brecon House
Stamford Road
Manchester
M16 4PL
Tel: 0161 521 6411
Fax: 0161 521 6412
Date: 14 April 20X1
Purchase order no: 7165

To: Haddow Bros
        The White House
        Standing Way
        Manchester
        M13 6FH

Delivery address
(If different from above)

-

Invoice address
(If different from above)

-

Code	Quantity	Description	Unit price (exclusive of VAT) £
PLY8FE1	12 sheets	Plywood Hardwood 2440 × 1220 mm	17.80

DELIVERY NOTE

Jenson Ltd

Deliver to:
Nethan Builders
Brecon House
Stamford Road
Manchester
M16 4PL

30 Longfield Park
Kingsway
M45 2TP
Tel: 0161 511 4666
Fax: 0161 511 4777

Delivery note no: 771460
Date: 19 April 20X1
VAT reg no: 641 3229 45

Code	Description	Quantity	VAT rate %	Unit price £	Amount exclusive of VAT £
PL432115	Door lining set 32 × 115 mm	14			
PL432140	Door lining set 32 × 138 mm	8			

Goods received in good condition.

Print name .... C JULIAN ....

Signature .... C Julian ....

Date .... 19/4/X1 ....

DELIVERY NOTE

A J Broom & Company Limited
59 Parkway
Manchester
M2 6EG
Tel: 0161 560 3392
Fax: 0161 560 5322

Deliver to:
Nethan Builders
Brecon House
Stamford Road
Manchester
M16 4PL

Delivery note no:	076429
Date:	20 April 20X1
VAT reg no:	661 2359 07
Purchase order no:	7164

Code	Description	Quantity	VAT rate %	Unit price £	Amount exclusive of VAT £
CIBF653	Joist hanger	7			
DGS472	SDG Softwood	9.6 m			

Goods received in good condition.

Print name ....C JULIAN...............

Signature .... *C Julian* ....

Date .... 20/4/X1 ....

DELIVERY NOTE

Haddow Bros

The White House
Standing Way
Manchester
M13 6FH
Tel: 0161 560 3140
Fax: 0161 560 6140

Deliver to:
Nethan Builders
Brecon House
Stamford Road
Manchester
M16 4PL

Delivery note no: 667713
Date: 17 April 20X1
VAT reg no: 460 3559 71

Code	Description	Quantity	VAT rate %	Unit price £	Amount exclusive of VAT £
PLY8FE1	Plywood Hardwood 2440 × 1220 mm	10			

Goods received in good condition.

Print name .... C JULIAN ....

Signature .... C Julian ....

Date .... 17/4/X1 ....

Chapter 14
Accounting for purchases – summary

QUESTION 46

Julian Hargreaves is a self-employed painter and decorator. He uses an analysed purchases day book and analyses his purchases into paints, wallpaper and other purchases.

Given below are three purchase invoices that he has received. The purchase ledger codes for the three suppliers are:

Mortimer & Co	PL03
F L Decor Supplies	PL06
Specialist Paint Ltd	PL08

Today's date is 22 March 20X1 and you are to enter these invoices into the analysed purchases day book given and total each of the columns.

INVOICE

Mortimer & Co

Invoice to:
Julian Hargreaves
28 Flynn Avenue
Corton
TN16 4SJ

Pearl Park Estate
Tonbridge
TN14 6LM
Tel: 01883 461207
Fax: 01883 461208

Deliver to:
As above

Invoice no:	047992
Tax point:	20 March 20X1
VAT reg no:	641 3299 07

Code	Description	Quantity	VAT rate %	Unit price £	Amount exclusive of VAT £
LP4882	Lining Paper Grade 2	40 rolls	17.5%	2.80	112.00
GL117	Wallpaper Glue	4 tins (2 litres)	17.5%	10.65	42.60
					154.60

VAT at 17.5%   26.37

Total amount payable   180.97

Deduct discount of 2½% if paid within 14 days

INVOICE

F L Decor Supplies

Invoice to:
Julian Hargreaves
28 Flynn Avenue
Corton
TN16 4SJ

64/66 Main Road
Flimfield
TN22 4HT
Tel: 01883 714206
Fax: 01883 714321

Deliver to:
As above

Invoice no:	61624
Tax point:	18 March 20X1
VAT reg no:	743 2116 05

Code	Description	Quantity	VAT rate %	Unit price £	Amount exclusive of VAT £
AG461	Anaglypta Wallpaper – White	16 rolls	17.5%	3.80	60.80
					60.80
Trade discount 10%					6.08
					54.72
VAT at 17.5%					9.57
Total amount payable					64.29

INVOICE

Invoice to:
Julian Hargreaves
28 Flynn Avenue
Corton
TN16 4SJ

Deliver to:
As above

Specialist Paint Ltd

Cedar House
Otford Way
Tonbridge
TN3 6AS
Tel: 01883 445511
Fax: 01883 445512

Invoice no:	05531
Tax point:	20 March 20X1
VAT reg no:	666 4557 28

Code	Description	Quantity	VAT rate %	Unit price £	Amount exclusive of VAT £
PT4168	Eggshell Paint – Fuchsia	6 tins (2 litres)	17.5%	16.40	98.40
BS118	Horse Hair Paint Brush 50 mm	10	17.5%	8.85	88.50
					186.90

VAT at 17.5%   32.21

Total amount payable   219.11

Deduct discount of 1.5% if paid within 10 days

Purchases day book

Date	Invoice no	Code	Supplier	Total	VAT	Paint	Wallpaper	Other

KAPLAN PUBLISHING

QUESTION 47

Given below is the purchases day book for a business for the week ending 12 March 20X1.

You are required to:

- prepare the journal entry for the posting of the totals to the main ledger – the last journal number was 0253;

- post the individual entries to the subsidiary ledger accounts given.

Purchases day book

Date	Invoice no	Code	Supplier	Total £	VAT £	01 £	02 £	03 £	04 £
08/3/X1	06121	PL12	Homer Ltd	223.87	33.34	68.90			121.63
	11675	PL07	Forker & Co	207.24	30.86		70.20	106.18	
09/3/X1	46251	PL08	Print Associates	230.04	34.26			64.88	130.90
10/3/X1	016127	PL02	ABG Ltd	292.58	43.57	118.60	130.41		
	C4366	PL07	Forker & Co	(23.73)	(3.53)		(20.20)		
11/3/X1	77918	PL19	G Greg	169.69	25.27	69.82		74.60	
	06132	PL12	Homer Ltd	189.33	28.19	70.24			90.90
12/3/X1	CN477	PL02	ABG Ltd	(48.31)	(7.19)	(16.80)	(24.32)		
				1,240.71	184.77	310.76	156.09	245.66	343.43

JOURNAL ENTRY	No:
Prepared by:	
Authorised by:	
Date:	
Narrative:	

Account	Debit	Credit
TOTALS		

Subsidiary ledger

ABG Ltd					PL02
£					£
		5/3	Balance b/d		486.90

Forker & Co					PL07
£					£
		5/3	Balance b/d		503.78

Print Associates					PL08
£					£
		5/3	Balance b/d		229.56

Homer Ltd					PL12
£					£
		5/3	Balance b/d		734.90

G Greg					PL19
£					£
		5/3	Balance b/d		67.89

QUESTION 48

Below you are given the purchases day book for a business for the week ending 24 February 20X1. You are required to:

- post the totals to the main ledger accounts given;
- post the individual entries to the subsidiary ledger accounts given.

Purchases day book

Date	Invoice no	Code	Supplier	Total	VAT	01	02	03	04
20/2/X1	46118	PL11	Fred Janitor	218.70	32.57	84.93		101.20	
	46119	PL07	S Doorman	189.53	28.22		86.51	74.80	
21/2/X1	46120	PL03	P & F Davis & Co	166.54	24.80	68.92	23.30		49.52
22/2/X1	CN462	PL11	Fred Janitor	(30.99)	(4.61)	(10.20)		(16.18)	
	46121	PL06	Clooney & Partner	230.58	34.34		87.54	60.08	48.62
23/2/X1	CN463	PL07	S Doorman	(21.51)	(3.20)		(18.31)		
24/2/X1	46122	PL03	P & F Davis & Co	189.23	28.18	78.40		82.65	
				942.08	140.30	222.05	179.04	302.55	98.14

Main ledger

Purchases ledger control account

		£			£
			17/2	Balance b/d	2,357.57

VAT account

		£			£
			17/2	Balance b/d	662.47

Purchases – 01 account

		£			£
17/2	Balance b/d	14,275.09			

Purchases - 02 account

		£			£
17/2	Balance b/d	12,574.26			

Purchases - 03 account

		£			£
17/2	Balance b/d	29,384.74			

Purchases – 04 account

		£			£
17/2	Balance b/d	9,274.36			

Subsidiary ledger

P & F Davis & Co — PL03

		£			£
			17/2	Balance b/d	368.36

Clooney & Partner — PL06

		£			£
			17/2	Balance b/d	226.48

S Doorman — PL07

		£			£
			17/2	Balance b/d	218.47

Fred Janitor — PL11

		£			£
			17/2	Balance b/d	111.45

QUESTION 49

Given below is the cheque payment listing for a business for the week ending 8 May 20X1.

Cheque payment listing				
Supplier	Code	Cheque number	Cheque amount £	Discount taken £
G Rails	PL04	001221	177.56	4.43
L Jameson	PL03	001222	257.68	7.73
Cash purchases		001223	216.43	
K Davison	PL07	001224	167.89	
T Ives	PL01	001225	289.06	5.79
Cash purchases		001226	263.78	
H Samuels	PL02	001227	124.36	

The cash purchases include VAT at the standard rate.

You are required to:

- enter the payments into the cash payments book given and total all of the columns;

- complete the journal for the posting of the totals to the main ledger – the last journal entry was number 1467;

- post the individual entries to the subsidiary ledger accounts given.

Cash payments book

Date	Details	Cheque no	Code	Total £	VAT £	Purchases ledger £	Cash purchases £	Other £	Discounts received £

JOURNAL ENTRY	No:		
Prepared by:			
Authorised by:			
Date:			
Narrative:			
Account		*Debit*	*Credit*
TOTALS			

Subsidiary ledger

	T Ives			*PL01*
	£			£
		1 May	Balance b/d	332.56

	H Samuels			*PL02*
	£			£
		1 May	Balance b/d	286.90

	L Jameson			*PL03*
	£			£
		1 May	Balance b/d	623.89

	G Rails			*PL04*
	£			£
		1 May	Balance b/d	181.99

	K Davison			*PL07*
	£			£
		1 May	Balance b/d	167.89

Chapter 15
Petty cash systems

QUESTION 50

Given below are the petty cash vouchers that have been paid during the week ending 12 January 20X1 out of a petty cash box run on an imprest system of £150 per week. At the end of each week a cheque requisition is drawn up for a cheque for cash to bring the petty cash box back to the imprest amount.

Voucher no	Amount £	Reason
03526	13.68	Postage
03527	25.00	Staff welfare
03528	14.80	Stationery (including £2.20 VAT)
03529	12.00	Taxi fare (including £1.79 VAT)
03530	6.40	Staff welfare
03531	12.57	Postage
03532	6.80	Rail fare
03533	7.99	Stationery (including £1.19 VAT)
03534	18.80	Taxi fare (including £2.80 VAT)

You are required to:

- write up the petty cash book given;

- prepare the cheque requisition for the cash required to restore the petty cash box to the imprest amount;

- post the petty cash book totals to the main ledger accounts given.

Petty cash book											
Receipts			**Payments**								
Date	Narrative	Total £	Date	Narrative	Voucher no	Total £	Postage £	Staff welfare £	Stationery £	Travel expenses £	VAT £

CHEQUE REQUISITION FORM

CHEQUE DETAILS

Date ....

Payee ....

Amount   £ ....

Reason ....

Invoice no. (attached/to follow) ....

Receipt (attached/to follow) ....

Required by   (Print) ....

(Signature) ....

Authorised by: ....

Main ledger accounts

Postage account

		£			£
5 Jan	Balance b/d	248.68			

Staff welfare account

		£			£
5 Jan	Balance b/d	225.47			

Stationery account

		£			£
5 Jan	Balance b/d	176.57			

Travel expenses account

		£			£
5 Jan	Balance b/d	160.90			

VAT account

		£			£
			5 Jan	Balance b/d	2,385.78

QUESTION 51

A business runs its petty cash on an imprest system with an imprest amount of £100 per week.

At the end of the week ending 22 May 20X1 the vouchers in the petty cash box were:

Voucher no	£
02634	13.73
02635	8.91
02636	10.57
02637	3.21
02638	11.30
02639	14.66

The cash remaining in the petty cash box was made up as follows:

£10 note	1
£5 note	2
£2 coin	3
£1 coin	7
50p coin	5
20p coin	4
10p coin	1
5p coin	2
2p coin	3
1p coin	6

You are required to reconcile the petty cash in the box to the vouchers in the box at 22 May 20X1 and if it does not reconcile to suggest reasons for the difference.

QUESTION 52

A business runs an imprest system with an imprest amount of £120. The rules of the petty cash system are as follows:

- only amounts of less than £30 can be paid out of petty cash, any larger claims must be dealt with by filling out a cheque requisition form;

- all petty cash claims over £5 must be supported by a receipt or invoice;

- the exception to this is that rail fares can be reimbursed without a receipt provided that the petty cash voucher is authorised by the department head;

- all other valid petty cash vouchers can be authorised by you, the petty cashier;

- all petty cash vouchers that are authorised are given a sequential number.

You have on your desk 10 petty cash vouchers which have been completed and you must decide which can be paid and which cannot.

PETTY CASH VOUCHER

Authorised by	Claimed by J Athersych		No	
Date	Description		Amount	
15/3/X1	Coffee		4	83
	Milk		1	42
	Biscuits		0	79
		Total	7	04

Receipt is attached.

PETTY CASH VOUCHER

Authorised by	Claimed by J Athersych		No	
Date	Description		Amount	
15/3/X1	Envelopes		4	85
		Total	4	85

No receipt.

PETTY CASH VOUCHER

Authorised by Department Head	Claimed by F Rivers		No	
Date	Description		Amount	
16/3/X1	Rail fare		12	80
		Total	12	80

No receipt.

PETTY CASH VOUCHER

Authorised by	Claimed by M Patterson	No	
Date	Description	Amount	
16/3/X1	Computer discs	4	20
	Printer paper	2	40
	Total	6	60

No receipt.

PETTY CASH VOUCHER

Authorised by	Claimed by D R Ray	No	
Date	Description	Amount	
17/3/X1	Lunch – entertaining clients	42	80
	Total	42	80

Bill attached.

PETTY CASH VOUCHER

Authorised by	Claimed by J Athersych	No	
Date	Description	Amount	
17/3/X1	Milk	1	42
	Tea bags	2	28
	Total	3	70

No receipt.

PETTY CASH VOUCHER

Authorised by	Claimed by D R Ray		No	
Date	Description		Amount	
18/3/X1	Rail fare		12	50
		Total	12	50

No receipt.

PETTY CASH VOUCHER

Authorised by	Claimed by M Patterson		No	
Date	Description		Amount	
18/3/X1	Special delivery postage		19	50
		Total	19	50

Receipt attached.

PETTY CASH VOUCHER

Authorised by	Claimed by M T Noble		No	
Date	Description		Amount	
18/3/X1	Ink for printer		17	46
		Total	17	46

Receipt attached.

```
┌─────────────────────────────────────────────────────────────┐
│                                                               │
│  ┌─────────────────────────────────────────────────────────┐ │
│  │                 PETTY CASH VOUCHER                        │ │
│  ├──────────────────┬──────────────────────────┬───────────┤ │
│  │ Authorised by    │ Claimed by               │ No        │ │
│  │                  │ J Norman                 │           │ │
│  ├──────────────────┼──────────────────────────┼───────────┤ │
│  │ Date             │ Description              │ Amount    │ │
│  ├──────────────────┼──────────────────────────┼─────┬─────┤ │
│  │ 18/3/X1          │ Rail fare                │  7  │ 60  │ │
│  ├──────────────────┼──────────────────────────┼─────┼─────┤ │
│  │                  │                          │     │     │ │
│  ├──────────────────┼──────────────────────────┼─────┼─────┤ │
│  │                  │                          │     │     │ │
│  ├──────────────────┼──────────────────────────┼─────┼─────┤ │
│  │                  │                          │     │     │ │
│  ├──────────────────┼──────────────────────────┼─────┼─────┤ │
│  │                  │                          │     │     │ │
│  ├──────────────────┴──────────────────────────┼─────┼─────┤ │
│  │                                        Total │  7  │ 60  │ │
│  └──────────────────────────────────────────────┴─────┴─────┘ │
└─────────────────────────────────────────────────────────────┘
```

No receipt.

QUESTION 53

A business runs its petty cash system on an imprest system with an imprest amount of £100 per week. During the week ended 30 April 20X1 the following petty cash vouchers were paid:

Voucher no	Amount £	Reason
002534	4.68	Coffee/milk
002535	13.26	Postage
002536	10.27	Stationery (including £1.53 VAT)
002537	15.00	Taxi fare (including £2.23 VAT)
002538	6.75	Postage
002539	7.40	Train fare
002540	3.86	Stationery (including £0.57 VAT)

You are required to:

• write up these vouchers in the petty cash book given;

• post the totals of the petty cash book to the main ledger accounts given.

Petty cash book

Receipts			Payments								
Date	Narrative	Total £	Date	Narrative	Voucher no	Total £	Postage £	Stationery £	Tea & coffee £	Travel £	VAT £

Main ledger accounts

Postage account

		£			£
23 April	Balance b/d	231.67			

Stationery account

		£			£
23 April	Balance b/d	334.78			

Tea and coffee account

		£			£
23 April	Balance b/d	55.36			

Travel expenses account

		£			£
23 April	Balance b/d	579.03			

VAT account

		£			£
			23 April	Balance b/d	967.44

QUESTION 54

SCENARIO

You are the cashier at Toybox Games Ltd, a manufacturer of children's board games. Part of your duties is the management of petty cash.

Personnel

Managing director	Andrew Pritchard

Department heads

Production director	Ian Grahamson
Buying director	Eric Connelly
Sales director	Derek Gibb
Management accountant	Sarah Chesterton

Accounts function

Accounts assistant	Andrew Donnelly
Credit controller	Stanley Green
Cashier	You

Procedures

Here is an extract from the group's procedures manual.

Petty cash

1   The main source of petty cash is cheques drawn on the main bank account. An imprest system is maintained. (Levels of cash held are set locally.)

2   Petty cash can only be paid out on the production of a petty cash voucher authorised by a department head.

In addition there are authorisation limits for each department head of £100.00. Any amount over £100.00 must be authorised by the managing director.

All petty cash vouchers over £5.00 must be supported by receipts/invoices (even if these are not proper VAT receipts/invoices).

Petty cash will not be paid out if the above rules are not followed.

3   Correctly completed petty cash vouchers must be numbered and correctly filed. If a voucher cannot be coded it must not be numbered or written up and the cash will not be paid.

4   Expenditure must be correctly coded and analysed in the petty cash book. The analysis must be performed at the same time as the petty cash book is written up.

VAT may only be reclaimed where the company holds a proper VAT invoice/receipt.

5   The petty cash book must be written up weekly. The balance of cash in hand must be reconciled to the records.

A cheque requisition must be completed for the balance needed to restore the level of cash held.

6   A journal must be prepared to post the totals of expenditure to the correct main ledger accounts.

Terms of trade

The company is registered for VAT. All sales of board games are standard-rated.

THE TASKS TO BE COMPLETED

Today is 4 December 20X1.

TASK 1   Produce a schedule of vouchers that cannot be paid, giving reasons for non-payment.

TASK 2   Write up the petty cash book to 30 November 20X1 from the acceptable vouchers provided. The last voucher before this batch was number 334.

TASK 3   Prepare a journal entry to post totals of expenditure to the correct ledger accounts. The last journal was number 3345.

PETTY CASH SCHEDULE OF CASH IN HAND AT 30 NOVEMBER 20X1

£10 notes	2
£5 notes	4
£1 coins	12
50p coins	1
20p coins	1
10p coins	1
2p coins	1

PETTY CASH VOUCHER				
Authorised by DG	Received by	Code	No	
Date	Description		Amount	
25/11	flowers for D Gibbs		16	99
	Secretary			
		Total	16	99

No receipt is available.

PETTY CASH VOUCHER

Authorised by SAC		Received by	Code	No	
Date	Description			Amount	
30/11	Coffee / tea			6	51
	Finance dept				
		Total		6	51

A receipt is available but it is not a proper VAT receipt.

PETTY CASH VOUCHER

Authorised by DG		Received by	Code	No	
Date	Description			Amount	
30/11	Biscuits / coffee / sugar			6	78
	Sales & Marketing				
	Kitchen				
		Total		6	78

A proper VAT receipt is available. VAT of 30 pence is recoverable.

PETTY CASH VOUCHER

Authorised by DG		Received by	Code	No	
Date	Description			Amount	
28/11	Coffee / milk			3	51
	Production				
		Total		3	51

KAPLAN PUBLISHING

PETTY CASH VOUCHER

Authorised by SAC		Received by	Code		No	
Date	Description			Amount		
28/11	Stamps -				3	68
	Finance dept (franking					
	machine empty)					
		Total			3	68

PETTY CASH VOUCHER

Authorised by DG		Received by	Code		No	
Date	Description			Amount		
27/11	Sales conference				12	99
	- Taxi home to station					
		Total			12	99

A receipt is available.

PETTY CASH VOUCHER

Authorised by EJC		Received by	Code		No	
Date	Description			Amount		
28/11	Food for staff party				13	71
	- Buying Department					
		Total			13	71

A proper VAT receipt is available - VAT of £1.50 reclaimable.

PETTY CASH VOUCHER

Authorised by DG	Received by		Code	No

Date	Description		Amount	
27/11	Sales conference		179	00
	- Rail tickets			
	Total		179	00

A receipt is available.

PETTY CASH VOUCHER

Authorised by IG	Received by		Code	No

Date	Description		Amount	
30/11	Window cleaner		7	00
	Total		7	00

A receipt is available. The window-cleaner is not registered for VAT. There is no code for this expense.

PETTY CASH VOUCHER

Authorised by	Received by		Code	No

Date	Description		Amount	
26/11	VAT Book -		15	78
	Finance Dept			
	Total		15	78

A receipt is available.

KAPLAN PUBLISHING

PETTY CASH BOOK

Date	Voucher number	£		£ 01 Sales		£ 02 Production		£ 03 Buying		£ 04 Finance		£ VAT		Code

JOURNAL   PETTY CASH EXPENDITURE   No

Prepared by _____   Week ending _____

Authorised by _____

Department	Expense	Account code	Debit	Credit
Sales / marketing	Entertainment	01 06 01 20		
	Education	21		
	Travelling	22		
	Welfare	23		
	Stationery/Post	24		
Production	Entertainment	01 06 02 20		
	Education	21		
	Travelling	22		
	Welfare	23		
	Stationery/Post	24		
Buying	Entertainment	01 06 03 20		
	Education	21		
	Travelling	22		
	Welfare	23		
	Stationery/Post	24		
Finance	Entertainment	01 06 04 20		
	Education	21		
	Travelling	22		
	Welfare	23		
	Stationery/Post	24		
VAT		02 08 90 00		
Petty cash		01 05 10 00		
TOTALS				

KAPLAN PUBLISHING

Chapter 16
Bank reconciliations

QUESTION 55

Given below are the cash receipts book, cash payments book and bank statement for a business for the week ending 11 March 20X1.

Required

- Compare the bank statement to the cash book.

- Correct the cash receipts and payments books for any items which are unmatched on the bank statement.

- Total the cash receipts book and cash payments book.

- Find the balance on the cash book if the opening balance on 7 March was £860.40 cash in hand.

- Explain why the amended cash book balance and the bank statement balance at 11 March are different.

Cash receipts book

Date	Narrative	Total £	VAT £	Debtors £	Other £	Discount £
20X1						
7/3	Paying in slip 0062	1,112.60	78.80	583.52	450.28	23.60
8/3	Paying in slip 0063	1,047.80	60.24	643.34	344.22	30.01
9/3	Paying in slip 0064	1,287.64	71.20	809.59	406.85	34.20
10/3	Paying in slip 0065	987.80	49.90	652.76	285.14	18.03
11/3	Paying in slip 0066	1,127.94	51.84	779.88	296.22	23.12

Cash payments book

Date	Details	Cheque No	Code	Total £	VAT £	Creditors £	Cash purchases £	Other £	Discounts received £
20X1									
7/3	P Barn	012379	PL06	383.21		383.21			
	Purchases	012380	ML	268.33	39.96		228.37		
	R Trevor	012381	PL12	496.80		496.80			6.30
8/3	F Nunn	012382	PL07	218.32		218.32			
	F Taylor	012383	PL09	467.28		467.28			9.34
	C Cook	012384	PL10	301.40		301.40			
9/3	L White	012385	PL17	222.61		222.61			
	Purchases	012386	ML	269.40	40.12		229.28		
	T Finn	012387	PL02	148.60		148.60			
10/3	S Penn	012388	PL16	489.23		489.23			7.41
11/3	P Price	012389	PL20	299.99		299.99			
	Purchases	012390	ML	264.49	39.39		225.10		

Bank statement

FINANCIAL BANK plc CONFIDENTIAL

You can bank on us!

10 Yorkshire Street Headingley Leeds LS1 1QT Telephone: 0113 633061	Account	CURRENT	Sheet 00614
	Account name	T R FABER LTD	

Statement date   11 March 20X1   Account Number   27943316

Date	Details	Withdrawals (£)	Deposits (£)	Balance (£)
7/3	Balance from sheet 00613			860.40
	Bank giro credit L Fernley		406.90	1,267.30
9/3	Cheque 012380	268.33		
	Cheque 012381	496.80		
	Credit 0062		1,112.60	1,614.77
10/3	Cheque 012383	467.28		
	Cheque 012384	301.40		
	Credit 0063		1,047.80	
	SO – Loan Finance	200.00		1,693.89
11/3	Cheque 012379	383.21		
	Cheque 012386	269.40		
	Cheque 012387	148.60		
	Credit 0064		1,287.64	
	Bank interest		6.83	2,187.15

SO	Standing order	DD	Direct debit	CP	Card purchase
AC	Automated cash	OD	Overdrawn	TR	Transfer

QUESTION 56

Given below is the cash book of a business and the bank statement for the week ending 20 April 20X1.

Required

Compare the cash book to the bank statement and note any differences that you find.

Cash book

Receipts		£	Payments		£
16/4	Donald & Co	225.47	16/4	Balance b/d	310.45
17/4	Harper Ltd	305.68	17/4	Cheque 03621	204.56
	Fisler Partners	104.67	18/4	Cheque 03622	150.46
18/4	Denver Ltd	279.57	19/4	Cheque 03623	100.80
19/4	Gerald Bros	310.45		Cheque 03624	158.67
20/4	Johnson & Co	97.68	20/4	Cheque 03625	224.67
			20/4	Balance c/d	173.91
		1,323.52			1,323.52

EXPRESS BANK

CONFIDENTIAL

You can bank on us!

High Street
Fenbury
TL4 6JY
Telephone: 0169 422130

Account	CURRENT	Sheet 0213
Account name	P L DERBY LTD	

Statement date   20 April 20X1 — Account Number   40429107

Date	Details	Withdrawals (£)	Deposits (£)	Balance (£)
16/4	Balance from sheet 0212			310.45 OD
17/4	DD – District Council	183.60		494.05 OD
18/4	Credit		225.47	268.58 OD
19/4	Credit		104.67	
	Cheque 03621	240.56		
	Bank interest	3.64		408.11 OD
20/4	Credit		305.68	
	Credit		279.57	
	Cheque 03622	150.46		
	Cheque 03624	158.67		131.99 OD

SO	Standing order	DD	Direct debit	CP	Card purchase	
AC	Automated cash	OD	Overdrawn	TR	Transfer	

KAPLAN PUBLISHING

QUESTION 57

Graham

The cash account of Graham showed a debit balance of £204 on 31 March 20X3. A comparison with the bank statements revealed the following:

			£
1	Cheques drawn but not presented		3,168
2	Amounts paid into the bank but not credited		723
3	Entries in the bank statements not recorded in the cash account		
	(i)	Standing orders	35
	(ii)	Interest on bank deposit account	18
	(iii)	Bank charges	14
4	Balance on the bank statement at 31 March		2,618

Tasks

(a) Show the appropriate adjustments required in the cash account of Graham bringing down the correct balance at 31 March 20X3.

(b) Prepare a bank reconciliation statement at that date.

QUESTION 58

Data

The following are the cash book and bank statements of Kiveton Cleaning.

Receipts June 20X1

CASH BOOK – JUNE 20X1				CB 117
Date	Details	Total	Sales ledger control	Other
1 June	Balance b/d	7,100.45		
8 June	Cash and cheques	3,200.25	3,200.25	-
15 June	Cash and cheques	4,100.75	4,100.75	-
23 June	Cash and cheques	2,900.30	2,900.30	-
30 June	Cash and cheques	6,910.25	6,910.25	-
		£24,212.00	£17,111.55	

Payments June 20X1

Date	Payee	Cheque no	Total	Purchase ledger control	Operating overhead	Admin overhead	Other
1 June	Hawsker Chemical	116	6,212.00	6,212.00			
7 June	Wales Supplies	117	3,100.00	3,100.00			
15 June	Wages and salaries	118	2,500.00		1,250.00	1,250.00	
16 June	Drawings	119	1,500.00				1,500.00
18 June	Blyth Chemical	120	5,150.00	5,150.00			
25 June	Whitby Cleaning Machines	121	538.00	538.00			
28 June	York Chemicals	122	212.00	212.00			
			£19,212.00	£15,212.00	£1,250.00	£1,250.00	£1,500.00

Crescent Bank plc
High Street
Sheffield

Statement no: 721

Page 1

Account: Alison Robb t/a Kiveton Cleaning

Account no: 57246661

Date	Details	Payments £	Receipts £	Balance £
20X1				
1 June	Balance b/fwd			8,456.45
1 June	113	115.00		8,341.45
1 June	114	591.00		7,750.45
1 June	115	650.00		7,100.45
4 June	116	6,212.00		888.45
8 June	CC		3,200.25	4,088.70
11 June	117	3,100.00		988.70
15 June	CC		4,100.75	5,089.45
15 June	118	2,500.00		2,589.45
16 June	119	1,500.00		1,089.45
23 June	120	5,150.00		4,060.55 O/D
23 June	CC		2,900.30	1,160.25 O/D

Key:

S/O	Standing Order	DD	Direct Debit
CC	Cash and cheques	CHGS	Charges
BACS	Bankers automated clearing	O/D	Overdrawn

Task

Examine the business cash book and the business bank statement shown in the data provided above. Prepare a bank reconciliation statement as at 30 June 20X1. Set out your reconciliation in the proforma below.

Proforma

BANK RECONCILIATION STATEMENT AS AT 30 JUNE 20X1

£

Balance per bank statement

Outstanding lodgements:

Unpresented cheques:

Balance per cash book   £

QUESTION 59

Task

Refer to the business cash book and the business bank statement reproduced below. You are required to perform a bank reconciliation as at 31 December 20X8. Set out your reconciliation in the proforma below.

CASH BOOK: RECEIPTS – DECEMBER 20X8

					CBR221
Date	Details	Total £	VAT £	Sales £	Other £
20X8					
01 Dec	Balance b/d	7,809.98			
01 Dec	Cash and cheques banked	5,146.02	710.58	4,060.44	375.00
08 Dec	Cash and cheques banked	4,631.42	689.79	3,941.63	
15 Dec	Cash and cheques banked	5,094.56	758.76	4,335.80	
23 Dec	Cash and cheques banked	6,488.47	966.37	5,522.10	
31 Dec	Cash and cheques banked	4,744.66	706.65	4,038.01	
		33,915.11	3,832.15	21,897.98	375.00

Note: The amount of £375 in the 'column is the proceeds on disposal of an item of fixtures and fittings.

CASHBOOK: PAYMENTS - DECEMBER 20X8

CBP221

Date	Payee	Cheque no	Total £	VAT £	Purchases ledger control £	Admin expenses £	Other £
20X8							
01 Dec	Morland Estates	17330	2,500.00			2,500.00	
01 Dec	Vitesse Cars	17331	5,000.00				5,000.00
03 Dec	Robin Toys Limited	17332	2,596.50		2,596.50		
07 Dec	Bonchester Land Ltd	17333	3,000.00			3,000.00	
09 Dec	Warner & Co	17334	1,500.00		1,500.00		
15 Dec	Brewer & Partners	17335	423.00	63.00		360.00	
15 Dec	Creative Play	17336	1,915.09		1,915.09		
16 Dec	Louise Montgomery	17337	800.00				800.00
22 Dec	Grain Studios	17338	2,393.86		2,393.86		
24 Dec	Carved Angels	17339	1,436.32		1,436.32		
29 Dec	Wages and salaries	17340	9,968.35			9,968.35	
31 Dec	Balance c/d		2,381.99				
			33,915.11	63.00	9,841.77	15,828.35	5,800.00
	Analysis						
	Rent					5,500.00	
	Office expenses					360.00	
	Wages and salaries					9,968.35	
	Motor vehicles: cost						5,000.00
	Drawings						800.00
	Total					15,828.35	5,800.00

Royal Westminster Bank plc

STATEMENT

28 High Street, Bonchester, BN3 7OT

50 – 66 – 11

Account: Cloudberry Crafts

Account no: 61324288

Statement no: 93

Date	Details	Payments £	Receipts £	Balance £
20X8				
01 Dec	Balance forward			7,069.75
01 Dec	CC		5,095.66	
01 Dec	17328	869.35		11,296.06
03 Dec	17325	1,619.42		9,676.64
07 Dec	CC		5,146.02	
07 Dec	17330	2,500.00		12,322.66
08 Dec	17329	1,866.66		10,456.00
09 Dec	CC		4,631.42	15,087.42
14 Dec	17331	5,000.00		
14 Dec	17333	3,000.00		7,087.42
16 Dec	CC		5,094.56	
16 Dec	17334	1,500.00		10,681.98
17 Dec	17332	2,596.50		8,085.48
20 Dec	17335	423.00		7,662.48
27 Dec	CC		6,488.47	14,150.95
29 Dec	17338	2,393.86		
29 Dec	17336	1,915.09		9,842.00

Key	S/O	Standing order
	DD	Direct debit
	CC	Cash and/or cheques
	CHGS	Charges
	BACS	Bankers automated clearing services
	O/D	Overdrawn

BANK RECONCILIATION STATEMENT – 31 DECEMBER 20X8

£

Balance per the cash book

Less items not yet credited

————

Add items not yet debited

————

Balance per bank statement

————

QUESTION 60

You are the cashier at Natural Products Ltd, a manufacturer of cosmetics. Your duties include writing up the cash book.

Today is 6 July 20X1.

TASK 1   Total the receipts and payments side of the cash book and determine the balance on the cash account if the balance at the start of the week was £84,579.77 in hand.

TASK 2   Post the totals of the cash receipts book and cash payments book to the main ledger accounts given.

TASK 3   Compare the cash book to the bank statement.

Take each item on the bank statement and then tick it when it is agreed to a cash book entry - also tick the cash book entry. Any cheques earlier than 389 will remain unticked on the bank statement in this example as the cash payments book does not go far enough back. (In practice these would be agreed to earlier pages in the cash payments book and therefore ticked.)

TASK 4   Send the cash book to your supervisor Caroline Everley with a memo documenting any errors found.

TASK 5   Calculate the revised balance on the cash book once the errors noted have been dealt with.

Note: You should keep a note of any errors you find to include in the memo in Task 4.

Cash book receipts

Date	Narrative	Paying in Slip	Total	Debtors	Mail order	VAT control	Discount allowed
26/6	Trade debtors	598	15,685.23	15,685.23			
	Mail order (Chq/PO)	599	386.29		328.76	57.53	
	Mail order (CC)	600	189.80		76.43	13.37	
27/6	Trade debtors	601	6,650.28	6,650.28			
	Mail order	602	115.98		98.71	17.27	
	Megastores plc	CHAPS	11,755.25	11,755.25			204.17
28/6	Trade debtors	603	12,223.81	12,223.81			
	Mail order	604	609.22		518.49	90.73	
29/6	Trade debtors	605	5,395.40	5,395.40			
	Mail order	606	98.60		83.91	14.69	
30/6	Trade debtors	607	2,641.68	2,641.68			
	Mail Order/shop	608	249.59		212.43	37.16	
29/6	Freeman Foods Group	CHAPS	14,776.04	14,776.04			256.64
30/6	Totals						

Cash book payments

Date	Narrative	Cheque	Total	Creditors	Salaries	Other	VAT control	Discount received
26/6	Blackwood Foodstuffs	389	325.99	325.99				
	Bruning & Soler	390	683.85	683.85				
	Dehlavi Kosmetatos	391	2,112.16	2,112.16				
	Environmentally Friendly Co Ltd	392	705.77	705.77				
	Greig Handling (Import)	393	1,253.98	1,253.98				
	Halpern Freedman	394	338.11	338.11				
	Kobo Design Studio	395	500.00	500.00				
	Rayner Food Co	396	375.22	375.22				
	Year 2000 Produce Co	397	1,100.68	1,100.68				
27/6	HM Customs & Excise	398	23,599.28				23,599.28	
28/6	Salaries - Bank Giro	400	48,995.63		48,995.63			
30/6	Arthur Chong Ltd	401	235.55	235.55				
	Dwyer & Co (Import)	402	469.55	469.55				23.48
	Earthworld Ltd	403	449.28	449.28				22.46
	English Electricity	DD	159.78			) 135.98	23.80	
	English Telecom	DD	224.47			() 191.04	33.43	
	Totals							

Main ledger accounts

Sales ledger control account

		£			£
24/6	Balance b/d	312,465.99			

Mail order sales account

		£			£
			24/6	Balance b/d	26,578.46

VAT control account

		£				£
			24/6	Balance b/d		29,375.32

Discount allowed account

		£			£
24/6	Balance b/d	4,627.56			

Purchases ledger control account

		£				£
			24/6	Balance b/d		25,476.34

Salaries account

		£		£
24/6	Balance b/d	105,374.36		

Electricity account

		£		£
24/6	Balance b/d	1,496.57		

Telephone account

		£		£
24/6	Balance b/d	967.47		

Discount received account

		£				£
			24/6	Balance b/d		336.58

FINANCIAL BANK PLC

CONFIDENTIAL

You can bank on us!

467 HIGH STREET   *Account*   CURRENT   *Sheet*   455
TAUNTON
TA1 9WE   *Account name*   NATURAL PRODUCTS LIMITED
Telephone
01832 722098

20X1   *Statement date:*   30 JUNE 20X1   *Account Number*   34786695

Date	Details		Withdrawals (£)	Deposits (£)	Balance (£)
27 JUN	Balance from sheet 454				11,305.11
27 JUN	MEGASTORES PLC	CHAPS		11,755.25	
	COUNTER CREDIT 591			13,604.01	
	COUNTER CREDIT 592			112.13	
	374		127.09		
	376		5,955.80		
	ENGLISH ELECTRIC	DD	159.78		30,533.83
28 JUN	COUNTER CREDIT 593			11,655.24	
	COUNTER CREDIT 594			683.11	
	COUNTER CREDIT 595			112.19	
	372		87.93		
	389		325.99		
	ENGLISH TELECOM	DD	224.47		42,345.98
29 JUN	COUNTER CREDIT 596			325.11	
	COUNTER CREDIT 597			60,331.90	
	391		2,112.16		
	382		331.80		
	FREEMAN FOODS GRP	CHAPS		14,776.04	
	COUNTER CREDIT 598			15,685.23	
	COUNTER CREDIT 599			386.29	
	COUNTER CREDIT 600			89.80	
	394		338.11		
	395		500.00		
	386		441.09		
	388		111.94		130,105.25
30 JUN	COUNTER CREDIT 601			6,650.28	
	COUNTER CREDIT 602			115.98	
	381		117.54		
	384		3,785.60		
	387		785.11		
	390		683.85		
	393		1,253.98		
	399		175.10		
	COUNTER CREDIT 603			12,223.81	
	COUNTER CREDIT 604			609.22	142,903.36

key   SO *Standing order*   DD *Direct debit*   CP *Card purchase*   AC *Automated cash*   OD *Overdrawn*
       CHAPS *Clearing House Automated Payments System*   BACS *Bankers Automated Clearing Service*

MEMORANDUM

To:

From:

Subject:

Date:

Chapter 17
Ledger balances and control accounts

QUESTION 61

Basil Spence is a dealer in fancy goods. At 1 January 20X9 his ledger included the following balances.

	£
Debtors	17,349
Creditors	16,593

The debtors at 1 January 20X9 were as follows:

	£
N Pevsner	5,700
R Hackney	5,823
The Prince of Wales Hotel	5,826

The creditors at 1 January 20X9 were as follows:

	£
E Lutyens	5,481
M Hutchinson	5,553
H Falkner	5,559

During January 20X9 Basil's books of prime entry showed the following:

Purchases day book	£		Sales day book	£
Lutyens	2,850		Pevsner	150
Hutchinson	2,055		Hackney	5,280
Falkner	3,360		Prince of Wales Hotel	4,995
	8,265			10,425

Cash payments book	£		Cash receipts book	£
Lutyens	2,700		Hackney	5,700
Hutchinson	150		Prince of Wales Hotel	5,826
Falkner	2,469			
	5,319			11,526

Hackney argued about £123 of his outstanding balance, saying that the goods concerned were of the wrong design. Basil decided to write off this amount.

Required

For the month of January 20X9, write up the:

(a) individual debtors' and creditors' accounts;
(b) sales ledger and purchases ledger control accounts;
(c) bad debt expense account;
(d) individual debtors' and creditors' listings.

QUESTION 62

The following totals are taken from the books of a business:

		£
1 January 20X1	Credit balance on purchases ledger control account	5,926
	Debit balance on sales ledger control account	10,268
31 January 20X1	Credit sales	71,504
	Credit purchases	47,713
	Cash received from credit customers	69,872
	Cash paid to creditors	47,028
	Sales ledger balances written off as bad	96
	Sales returns	358
	Purchases returns	202
	Discounts allowed	1,435
	Discounts received	867
	Contra entry	75

Required

(a)   Prepare the purchases ledger control account and balance at the end of the month.

(b)   Prepare the sales ledger control account and balance at the end of the month.

QUESTION 63

The purchases ledger control account of Birkett is as follows:

Purchases ledger control account

	£		£
Purchase returns	13,418	Balance b/f	84,346
Cash book	525,938	Purchases (purchases	
Balance c/f	97,186	day book)	552,196
	———		———
	636,542		636,542
	———		———
		Balance b/f	97,186

Balances extracted from the purchases ledger totalled £96,238.

The following errors have been discovered.

1   The purchases day book was undercast by £6,000.

2   A cash account total of £10,858 was posted to the control account as £9,058.

3   A credit balance of £1,386 on the purchases ledger had been set off against a sales ledger debit balance but no entry had been made in the control accounts (a contra entry).

4   A debit balance of £40 in the list of purchases ledger balances had been extracted as a credit balance.

5   A credit balance of £3,842 had been omitted from the list of balances.

Required

(a)   Correct the control account.

(b)   Reconcile the adjusted account with the sum of the balances extracted.

QUESTION 64

The balance on the sales ledger control account of Robin & Co on 30 September 20X0 amounted to £3,825 which did not agree with the net total of the list of sales ledger balances at that date of £3,362.

The errors discovered were as follows:

1   Debit balances in the sales ledger, amounting to £103, had been omitted from the list of balances.

2   A bad debt amounting to £400 had been written off in the sales ledger but had not been posted to the bad debts expense account or entered in the control accounts.

3   An item of goods sold to Sparrow, £250, had been entered once in the sales day book but posted to his account twice.

4   No entry had been made in the control account in respect of the transfer of a debit of £70 from Quail's account in the sales ledger to his account in the purchases ledger (a contra entry).

5   The discount allowed column in the cash account had been undercast by £140.

Required

(a)   Make the necessary adjustments in the sales ledger control account and bring down the balance.

(b)   Show the adjustments to the net total of the original list of balances to reconcile with the amended balance on the sales ledger control account.

QUESTION 65

When carrying out the sales ledger control account reconciliation the following errors were discovered:

(a)   a bad debt of £800 had been written off in the subsidiary ledger but not in the main ledger;

(b)   a contra entry of £240 had been made in the subsidiary ledger but not in the main ledger;

(c)   the discount allowed column in the cash receipts book had been undercast by £100.

Required

Produce journal entries to correct each of these errors.

QUESTION 66

When carrying out the purchases ledger control account reconciliation the following errors were discovered:

(a)   the purchases day book was overcast by £1,000;

(b)   the total of the discount received column in the cash payments book was posted to the main ledger as £89 instead of £98;

(c)   a contra entry of £300 had been entered in the subsidiary ledger but not in the main ledger.

Required

Produce journal entries to correct each of these errors.

Chapter 18
Drafting an initial trial balance

QUESTION 67

Given below are the balances of a business at 31 May 20X1.

	£
Purchases	385,800
Creditors	32,000
Computer	8,000
Motor car	19,200
Discount received	3,850
Telephone	4,320
Sales returns	6,720
Wages	141,440
VAT (credit balance)	7,200
Drawings	60,000
Discount allowed	6,400
Rent and rates	26,200
Debtors	53,500
Motor expenses	7,700
Sales	642,080
Stock	38,880
Inland Revenue	3,800
Purchases returns	2,560
Electricity	6,080
Bank (debit balance)	1,920
Capital	74,670

Required

Prepare the trial balance as at 31 May 20X1.

QUESTION 68

Given below are the ledger accounts for the first month of trading for a small business.

Capital account

		£			£
			1 Mar	Bank	12,000

Bank account

		£			£
1 Mar	Capital	12,000	2 Mar	Motor car	4,500
7 Mar	Sales	3,000	2 Mar	Purchases	2,400
20 Mar	Sales	2,100	14 Mar	Rent	600
26 Mar	Debtors	3,800	18 Mar	Stationery	200
			25 Mar	Creditors	3,100
			28 Mar	Drawings	1,600

Motor car account

		£			£
2 Mar	Bank	4,500			

Purchases account

		£			£
2 Mar	Bank	2,400			
4 Mar	Creditors	2,500			
12 Mar	Creditors	4,100			

Creditors' account

		£			£
25 Mar	Bank	3,100	4 Mar	Purchases	2,500
			12 Mar	Purchases	4,100

Sales account

		£			£
			7 Mar	Bank	3,000
			10 Mar	Debtors	4,600
			15 Mar	Debtors	3,500
			20 Mar	Bank	2,100

Debtors' account

		£			£
10 Mar	Sales	4,600	26 Mar	Bank	3,800
15 Mar	Sales	3,500			

Rent account

		£			£
14 Mar	Bank	600			

Stationery account

		£			£
18 Mar	Bank	200			

Drawings account

		£			£
28 Mar	Bank	1,600			

Required

Balance off the ledger accounts and produce a trial balance at the end of the first month of trading.

QUESTION 69

Given below is a list of the balances for a business at the end of June 20X1.

	£
Debtors	33,440
Bank (debit balance)	1,200
Sales	401,300
Stock	24,300
Wages	88,400
Telephone	2,700
Motor car	12,000
VAT (credit balance)	7,000
Electricity	3,800
Rent	16,400
Purchases	241,180
Purchases returns	1,600
Sales returns	4,200
Office equipment	5,000
Capital	49,160
Motor expenses	4,840
Discounts allowed	4,010
Discounts received	2,410
Creditors	20,000
Drawings	40,000

Required

Draw up the trial balance at 30 June 20X1.

QUESTION 70

Introduction

Music World Ltd operates as a wholesaler supplying cassette tapes and compact discs throughout the UK.

The managing director is Jane Alder whilst Tony Bryant is the accountant and company secretary. You are employed as a bookkeeper to assist Tony Bryant.

Data

The following transactions all occurred on 1 December 20X1 and have been entered for you into summarised books of original entry. VAT has been calculated to the nearest pound at a rate of 17.5% and you should continue to use this rate for any subsequent calculations.

Treat 'other customers' and 'other suppliers' as individual accounts.

Sales day book

	Total £	VAT £	Net £
Hit Records Ltd	4,279	637	3,642
Smiths & Co	6,023	897	5,126
Classic Music	1,978	295	1,683
Other customers	12,307	1,833	10,474
	24,587	3,662	20,925

Purchases day book

	Total £	VAT £	Net £	Goods for resale £	Heating & lighting £
HMI Ltd	10,524	1,567	8,957	8,957	
Atlantic Imports Ltd	12,528	1,866	10,662	10,662	
Southern Electric	606	90	516		516
Other suppliers	5,652	842	4,810	4,810	
	29,310	4,365	24,945	24,429	516

Sales returns day book

	Total £	VAT £	Net £
Classic Music	167	25	142

Purchases returns day book

	Total £	VAT £	Net £
Atlantic Imports Ltd	32	5	27

Cash book

		£
Opening balance at start of day		14,492 (debit)

Receipts	Discount £	Amount received £	
Classic Music	45	1,755	
		———	
			1,755
			———
			16,247

Payments	Discount £	Total amount paid £	VAT £	
Atlantic Imports Ltd	112	4,388		
Equipment purchased		970	144	
Equipment repairs		102	15	
Unpaid cheque – Classic Music		1,000		
Bank charges		67		
Cash purchases		230	34	
Other suppliers		10,565		
		———		
				17,322
Closing balance at end of day				1,075 (credit)
				———

The following balances are available to you at the start of the day on 1 December 20X1:

	£
Customers:	
Hit Records Ltd	10,841
Smiths & Co	18,198
Classic Music	16,742
Other customers	491,702
Suppliers:	
HMI Ltd	82,719
Atlantic Imports Ltd	43,607
Southern Electric	Nil
Other suppliers	278,220
Other:	
Purchases	2,432,679
Sales	3,284,782
Sales returns	10,973
Purchases returns	9,817
Heating and lighting	1,728
Equipment	4,182
Equipment repairs	166
Bank charges	82
VAT (credit balance)	63,217
Discount allowed	11,420
Discount received	8,516
Sales ledger control account	537,483
Purchases ledger control account	404,546
Various other debit balances – total	1,368,815
Various other credit balances – total	611,142

THE TASKS TO BE COMPLETED

Complete all the following tasks.

TASK 1 Enter the opening balances into the following accounts on the ledger sheets provided.

> Sales ledger control account
> Purchases ledger control account
> Equipment
> Heating and lighting
> Purchases
> VAT
> Classic Music
> Atlantic Imports Ltd

TASK 2 Enter all relevant entries into the accounts shown in Task 1.

TASK 3 Balance off all the accounts in which you have made entries in Task 2.

TASK 4 Calculate the closing balances of the remaining accounts. Complete the list of balances given by inserting the updated figure for each account in either the debit balances column or the credit balances column as appropriate. Total the two columns. The two totals should be the same. If they do not agree try to trace and correct any errors you have made within the time you have available. If you are still unable to make the totals balance, leave the work incomplete.

Note: It is not a requirement to draw up all the individual accounts in order to calculate the closing balances for Task 4. Candidates may, however, adopt that approach if they wish.

Main ledger

Sales ledger control account

Date	Details	Amount £	Date	Details	Amount £

Purchases ledger control account

Date	Details	Amount £	Date	Details	Amount £

Equipment

Date	Details	Amount £	Date	Details	Amount £

Heating and lighting

Date	Details	Amount £	Date	Details	Amount £

Purchases

Date	Details	Amount £	Date	Details	Amount £

VAT

Date	Details	Amount £	Date	Details	Amount £

Subsidiary (sales) ledger

Classic Music

Date	Details	Amount £	Date	Details	Amount £

Subsidiary (purchases) ledger

Atlantic Imports Ltd

Date	Details	Amount £	Date	Details	Amount £

List of updated balances at the end of the day:

	Debit balances £	Credit balances £
Customers:		
Hit Records Ltd	....	....
Smiths & Co	....	....
Classic Music	....	....
Other customers	....	....
Suppliers:		
HMI Ltd	....	....
Atlantic Imports Ltd	....	....
Southern Electric	....	....
Other suppliers	....	....
Other:		
Purchases	....	....
Sales	....	....
Sales returns	....	....
Purchases returns	....	....
Heating and lighting	....	....
Equipment	....	....
Equipment repairs	....	....
Bank charges	....	....
VAT	....	....
Bank	....	....
Discount allowed	....	....
Discount received	....	....
Other debit balances	1,368,815	....
Other credit balances	....	611,142
	————	————
Totals		
	————	————

KAPLAN PUBLISHING

Chapter 19
Final Accounts and Accounting Concepts

Trading and Profit and Loss Account for Period Ending Date Month Year

	£	£
Sales		xxx.xx
Opening stock	xx.xx	
Add purchases	xx.xx	
	xx.xx	
Less closing stock	(xx.xx)	
Cost of goods		(xx.xx)
Gross profit		xxx.xx

Here you can see that the opening stock is added to purchases and then the value of closing stock is deducted to determine cost of sales, the cost of sales is deducted from sales to determine gross profit. We then continue the statement:-

Expenses:-

Repair and Maintenance	xx.xx	
Motor Vehicle running costs	xx.xx	
Insurances	xx.xx	
Office Expenses	xx.xx	
Wages and Salaries	xx.xx	
Depreciation	xx.xx	
		(xx.xx)
Net profit for year		xxx.xx

The total expenses are deduced are deducted from the gross profit to give net profit for the year.

A typical Balance Sheet would show:-

Balance Sheet as at Date Month Year

Fixed Assets   £

Tools & Equipment   xx.xx

Motor Vehicle   xx.xx

Office Equipment   xx.xx

                                                               xxx.xx

(Note here that the fixed assets are sub-totalled).

Current Assets

Stocks   xx.xx

Debtors   xx.xx

Cash   xx.xx

Bank   xx.xx

                                                               xxx.xx

(Note here current assets are sub totalled).

Less Current Liabilities

Creditors   xx.xx

VAT   xx.xx

Net current assets   (xxx.xx)

(Note this is current assets less current liabilities).

Total assets Less Current liabilities   xxx.xx

(Note here is fixed assets plus net current assets).

Less Long Term Liability

Loan   (xx.xx)

Net assets   xxx.xx

(Note this is total assets less current liabilities less the long term liability).

KAPLAN PUBLISHING

Financed by:-

Capital at start	xx.xx
Add profit for year	xx.xx
Less drawings	(xx.xx)
	xxx.xx
	=====

This completes the accounting equation.

Illustration 1 (with answers)

Tony Brown is a self employed joiner.

This Trial Balance as at 31 March 2007 showed:-

	Dr	Cr
Capital		30,000
Bank Loan		4,500
Motor Vehicles	17,000	
Tools and Equipment	19,600	
Office Equipment	4,000	
Stocks Materials	1,500	
Bank	1,280	
Cash	100	
Debtors	3,600	
Creditors		2,100
VAT Account		800
Sales (work done)		80,000
Purchases (materials)	34,500	
Repairs and Maintenance	1,520	
Motor Vehicle Running Costs	3,450	
Insurances	1,250	
Office Expenses	600	
Wages	8,000	
Drawings	21,000	
	117,400	117,400
	======	======

Closing stock @ 31 March 2007 £1,620

Answer

Tony Brown Trading and Profit and Loss Account for year ended 31 March 2007

	£	£
Sales (work done)		80,000
Opening Stock (materials)	1,500	
Add purchases	34,500	
	36,000	
Less stocks at 31 March 2007	1,620	
Cost of materials used		34,380
Gross profit		45,620
Expenses:-		
Repairs Maintenance	1,520	
Motor Vehicle Running Costs	3,450	
Insurances	1,250	
Office Expenses	600	
Wages	8,000	
		14,820
Net profit for year		30,800

Balance Sheet as at 31 March 2007

	£	£
Fixed Assets		
Tools and Equipment	19,600	
Motor Vehicle	17,000	
Office Equipment	4,000	
		40,600
Current Assets		
Stocks	1,620	
Debtors	3,600	
Cash	100	
Bank	1,280	
	6,600	
Less Current Liabilities		
Creditors	2,100	
VAT	800	
	2,900	
Net Current Assets		3,700
Total Assets Less Current Liabilities		44,300
Less Long Term Liabilities		
Loan		4,500
Net Assets		39,800
		=====
Financed by:-		
Capital		30,000
Add profit for year		30,800
		60,800
Less Drawings		(21,000)
		39,800
		=====

KAPLAN PUBLISHING

QUESTION 71

John Risdon is a self-employed plumber and his trial balance as at 31 March 2007 showed:-

	Dr	Cr
Capital		36,000
Bank Loan		6,500
Motor Vehicle	18,500	
Tools and Equipment	20,000	
Office Equipment	5,000	
Stocks Materials	1,750	
Bank	4,000	
Cash	450	
Debtors	4,100	
Creditors		2,600
VAT Account		1,000
Sales (work done)		84,500
Purchases Materials)	38,100	
Repairs and Maintenance	1,750	
Insurance	1,400	
Motor Vehicle Running Costs	4,100	
Office Expenses	700	
Wages	8,750	
Drawings	22,000	
	130,600	130,600

Stocks of materials as at 31 March 2007-07-30

Task

Prepare the Trading and Profit and Loss Account for year ended 31 March 2007 together with a Balance Sheet as that date.

QUESTION 72

Andrew Fewster is a self employed painter and decorator his trial balance as at 31 March 2007 showed:-

	Dr	Cr
Capital		37,500
Bank Loan		10,500
Motor Vehicle	22,500	
Tools and Equipment	21,000	
Office Equipment	5,500	
Stocks of Materials	1,950	
Bank	1,000	
Cash	200	
Debtors	5,500	
Creditors		2,950
VAT Account		1,400
Sales (work done)		86,500
Purchases (materials)	39,500	
Repairs and Maintenance	1,950	
Motor Vehicles Running Costs	4,250	
Insurance	1,850	
Office Expenses	950	
Wages	9,200	
Drawings	23,500	
	138,850	138,850

Stocks of materials at 31 March 2007 £2,150.

Depreciation is to be provided on:-
Motor Vehicles £5,625, Tools and Equipment £5,250 and Office Equipment £1,375

Insurance are prepaid and office expenses are accrued £250 and £50 respectively.

Prepare the final accounts for year ended 31 March 2007.

Chapter 20
Capital expenditure and revenue expenditure
QUESTION 73

Stapling machine

When a company purchases a new stapler so that accounts clerks can staple together relevant pieces of paper, the amount of the purchase is debited to the fittings and equipment (cost) account.

(a)   Is this treatment correct?

(b)   If so, why; if not, why not?

QUESTION 74

Office equipment

A company bought a small item of computer software costing £32.50. This had been treated as office equipment. Do you agree with this treatment? Give brief reasons.

QUESTION 75

Engine

If one of a company's vans had to have its engine replaced at a cost of £1,800, would this represent capital or revenue expenditure? Give brief reasons.

QUESTION 76

Included in the motor expenses of £4,134 is £2,000 paid by Simple Station for a motor vehicle which is being purchased under a hire purchase agreement.

When should Simple Station record the motor vehicle as a fixed asset in the books of the business?

(Note: You should circle the most appropriate answer.)

- When the first instalment is paid.
- When the final instalment is paid.
- The motor vehicle is never shown as a fixed asset.

Chapter 21
Depreciation

QUESTION 77

Mead is a sole trader with a 31 December year end. He purchased a car on 1 January 20X3 at a cost of £12,000. He estimates that its useful life is four years, after which he will trade it in for £2,400. The annual depreciation charge is to be calculated using the straight line method.

Task
Write up the motor car cost and provision for depreciation accounts and the depreciation expense account for the first three years, bringing down a balance on each account at the end of each year

QUESTION 78

S Telford purchases a machine for £6,000. He estimates that the machine will last eight years and its scrap value then will be £1,000.

Tasks

(1)   Prepare the machine cost and provision for depreciation accounts for the first three years of the machine's life, and show the balance sheet extract at the end of each of these years charging depreciation on the straight line method.

(2)   What would be the net book value of the machine at the end of the third year if depreciation was charged at 20% on the reducing balance method?

QUESTION 79

Hillton

(a)   Hillton started a veggie food manufacturing business on 1 January 20X6. During the first three years of trading he bought machinery as follows:

January	20X6	Chopper	Cost	£4,000
April	20X7	Mincer	Cost	£6,000
June	20X8	Stuffer	Cost	£8,000

Each machine was bought for cash.

Hillton's policy for machinery is to charge depreciation on the straight line basis at 25% per annum. A full year's depreciation is charged in the year of purchase, irrespective of the actual date of purchase.

Required

For the three years from 1 January 20X6 to 31 December 20X8 prepare the following ledger accounts:

(i)   Machinery account
(ii)   Provision for depreciation account (machinery)
(iii)   Depreciation expense account (machinery)

Bring down the balance on each account at 31 December each year.

Tip – Use a table to calculate the depreciation charge for each year.

KAPLAN PUBLISHING

(b)   Over the same three year period Hillton bought the following motor vehicles for his business:

January 20X6	Metro van	Cost	£3,200
July 20X7	Transit van	Cost	£6,000
October 20X8	Astra van	Cost	£4,200

Each vehicle was bought for cash.

Hillton's policy for motor vehicles is to charge depreciation on the reducing balance basis at 40% per annum. A full year's depreciation is charged in the year of purchase, irrespective of the actual date of purchase.

Required

For the three years from 1 January 20X6 to 31 December 20X8 prepare the following ledger accounts:

(i)   Motor vehicles account
(ii)   Provision for depreciation account (motor vehicles)
(iii)   Depreciation expense account (motor vehicles)

Bring down the balance on each account at 31 December each year.

Tip – Use another depreciation table.

QUESTION 80

On 1 December 20X2 Infortec Computers owned motor vehicles costing £28,400. During the year ended 30 November 20X3 the following changes to the motor vehicles took place:

		£
1 March 20X3	Sold vehicle – original cost	18,000
1 June 20X3	Purchased new vehicle – cost	10,000
1 September 20X3	Purchased new vehicle – cost	12,000

Depreciation on motor vehicles is calculated on a monthly basis at 20% per annum on cost.

Complete the table below to calculate the total depreciation charge to profits for the year ended 30 November 20X3.

	£
Depreciation for vehicle sold 1 March 20X3	....
Depreciation for vehicle purchased 1 June 20X3	....
Depreciation for vehicle purchased 1 September 20X3	....
Depreciation for other vehicles owned during the year	....
Total depreciation for the year ended 30 November 20X3	....

Chapter 22

Accruals and prepayments

QUESTION 81

Siobhan

Siobhan, the proprietor of a sweet shop, provides you with the following information in respect of sundry expenditure and income of her business for the year ended 31 December 20X4:

1   **Rent payable**

£15,000 was paid during 20X4 to cover the 15 months ending 31 March 20X5.

2   **Gas**

£840 was paid during 20X4 to cover gas charges from 1 January 20X4 to 31 July 20X4. Gas charges can be assumed to accrue evenly over the year. There was no outstanding balance at 1 January 20X4.

3   **Advertising**

Included in the payments totalling £3,850 made during 20X4 is an amount of £500 payable in respect of a planned campaign for 20X5.

4   **Bank interest**

The bank statements of the business show that the following interest has been charged to the account.

For period up to 31 May 20X4	Nil (no overdraft)
For 1 June – 31 August 20X4	£28
1 September – 30 November 20X4	£45

The bank statements for 20X5 show that £69 was charged to the account on 28 February 20X5.

5   **Rates**

Towards the end of 20X3 £4,800 was paid to cover the six months ended 31 March 20X4.

In May 20X4 £5,600 was paid to cover the six months ended 30 September 20X4.

In early 20X5 £6,600 was paid for the six months ending 31 March 20X5.

6   **Rent receivable**

During 20X4, Siobhan received £250 rent from Joe Soap for the use of a lock-up garage attached to the shop, in respect of the six months ended 31 March 20X4.

She increased the rent to £600 pa from 1 April 20X4, and during 20X4 Joe Soap paid her rent for the full year ending 31 March 20X5.

Required

Write up ledger accounts for each of the above items, showing:

(a)   the opening balance at 1 January 20X4, if any.
(b)   any cash paid or received.
(c)   the closing balance at 31 December 20X4.
(d)   the charge or credit for the year to the profit and loss account.

QUESTION 82

A Crew

The following is an extract from the trial balance of A Crew at 31 December 20X1:

	Dr £
Stationery	560
Rent	900
Rates	380
Lighting and heating	590
Insurance	260
Wages and salaries	2,970

Stationery which had cost £15 was still in hand at 31 December 20X1.

Rent of £300 for the last three months of 20X1 had not been paid and no entry has been made in the books for it.

£280 of the rates was for the year ended 31 March 20X2. The remaining £100 was for the three months ended 31 March 20X1.

Fuel had been delivered on 18 December 20X1 at a cost of £15 and had been consumed before the end of 20X1. No invoice had been received for the £15 fuel in 20X1 and no entry has been made in the records of the business.

£70 of the insurance paid was in respect of insurance cover for the year 20X2.

Nothing was owing to employees for wages and salaries at the close of 20X1.

Required

Record the above information in the relevant accounts, showing the transfers to the profit and loss account for the year ended 31 December 20X1.

QUESTION 83

A Metro

A Metro owns a number of antique shops and, in connection with this business, he runs a small fleet of motor vans. He prepares his accounts to 31 December in each year.

On 1 January 20X0 the amount prepaid for motor tax and insurance was £570.

On 1 April 20X0 he paid £420 which represented motor tax on six of the vans for the year ended 31 March 20X1.

On 1 May 20X0 he paid £1,770 insurance for all ten vans for the year ended 30 April 20X1.

On 1 July 20X0 he paid £280 which represented motor tax for the other four vans for the year ended 30 June 20X1.

Required

Write up the account for 'motor tax and insurance' for the year ended 31 December 20X0.

Chapter 23
VAT

QUESTION 84

You work as a bookkeeper for a small firm of accountants. Much of your work centres on small and medium sized sole traders and partnerships. You are often involved with the preparation of VAT returns for small businesses.

When accepting new clients you are often asked what records the Customs and Excise require a registered business to keep.

Prepare a checklist of such detail which you can give to clients in answer to this question.

QUESTION 85

The following are commonly used VAT terms:

- Supply of goods
- Supply of services
- Output tax
- Input tax
- Zero rated item
- Exempt item
- Standard rated

Define clearly each of the above VAT terms.

QUESTION 86

The Customs and Excise do not specify a standard format of invoice for registered businesses. However, there are certain essential elements to be shown on a VAT invoice.

List these, explaining clearly the purpose of each.

QUESTION 87

Some businesses, particularly retailers, are permitted to issue a 'less detailed tax invoice'.

List the elements which need to be shown on this type of document.

QUESTION 88

You are a self-employed bookkeeper and Duncan Bye, a motor engineer, is one of your clients. He is registered for VAT with registration number 131 7250 19.

His records for the quarter ended 30 June 20X1 showed the following:

Sales day book

	Gross £	Net £	VAT £
April	7,931.25	6,750.00	1,181.25
May	7,649.25	6,510.00	1,139.25
June	9,682.00	8,240.00	1,442.00
	25,262.50	21,500.00	3,762.50

Purchases day book

	Gross £	Net £	VAT £
April	3,701.25	3,150.00	551.25
May	3,842.25	3,270.00	572.25
June	3,149.00	2,680.00	469.00
	10,692.50	9,100.00	1,592.50

He also gives you some details of petty cash expenditure in the quarter.

	£
Net purchases	75.60
VAT	13.23
	88.83

He informs you that he used some parts on a job to repair his own car. The parts had previously cost him £120 (exclusive of VAT).

Prepare the following VAT form 100 for the period, ready for Duncan Bye's signature.

Value Added Tax Return

For the period

HM Customs
and Excise

Fold Here

For Official Use

Registration number | Period

You could be liable to a financial penalty if your completed return and all the VAT payable are not received by the due date.

Due date:

For official use D O R only

Before you fill in this form read the notes on the back and the VAT leaflet *'Filling in your VAT Return'*. Fill in all boxes clearly in ink, and write 'none' where necessary. Don't put a dash or leave any box blank. If there are no pence write '00' in the pence column. **Do not** enter more than one amount in any box.

For official use			£	p
	VAT due in this period on **sales** and other outputs	1		
	VAT due in this period on **acquisitions** from other **EC Member States**	2		
	Total VAT due (**the sum of boxes 1 and 2**)	3		
	VAT reclaimed in this period on **purchases** and other inputs (including acquisitions from the EC)	4		
	Net VAT to be paid to Customs or reclaimed by you (Difference between boxes 3 and 4)	5		
	Total value of **sales** and all other outputs excluding any VAT. **Include your box 8 figure.**	6		00
	Total value of **purchases** and all other inputs excluding any VAT. **Include your box 9 figure.**	7		00
	Total value of all **supplies** of goods and related services, excl any VAT, to other **EC Member States.**	8		00
	Total value of all **acquisitions** of goods and related servs, excl any VAT, from other **EC Member States.**	9		00

Retail schemes. If you have used any of the schemes in the period covered by this return, enter the relevant letter(s) in this box.

If you are enclosing a payment please tick this box.

DECLARATION: You, or someone on your behalf, must sign below.
I, ... declare that the
(Full name of signatory in BLOCK LETTERS)
information given above is true and complete.
Signature... Date .... 20.............

A false declaration can result in prosecution.

VAT 100 (Full)

PCU (June 1996)

This scenario based question is divided into two tasks, and contains a large amount of data which you may need to complete the tasks. You are advised to read the whole of the material before commencing the tasks.

You are provided with proforma schedules and report forms for the tasks and these are included at the end of the question.

The situation

Business: Daniel and James, Licensed Bookkeeper

Personnel: Partners – James Musgrave and Daniel Robb
Bookkeeper – you
Junior technician – Brenda Peach
Administration assistant – Diane Kelly

Data and tasks

Your work involves bookkeeping and accounting services mainly to small businesses.

Mark Ambrose is one of your clients; he is a self-employed master joiner and this assessment focuses on his file. The time is mid October 20X1.

Tasks to be completed

Task 1

Refer to the memo from James Musgrave below, immediately following the Tasks, regarding Mark Ambrose, and prepare the VAT form for the quarter ended 30 September 20X1 – a blank VAT form is provided at the end of the question.

Task 2

Write a letter to Mark Ambrose enclosing his VAT return for signature and explain to him how you have dealt with the VAT on the bad debts listed on his schedule, and also the private use of the materials.

Write your letter on the blank notepaper provided at the end of the question.

Data

MEMO

To: Bookkeeper

From: James Musgrave

Date: 15 October 20X1

Subject: Mark Ambrose - VAT return and query

I attach a letter and details relating to Mark's VAT return for quarter ended 30 September 20X1.

Could you please complete the form, incorporating any necessary adjustments for VAT on bad debts queried in his letter.

Many thanks.

James

Mark Ambrose
Master Joiner
High Park House
High Melton
Doncaster   DN5 7EZ

13 October 20X1

Dear James

I attach two schedules you will need for completing my VAT return for this quarter.

I have suffered some loss from bad debts in recent months and would like you to claim back the VAT on these – if that is possible.

I look forward to hearing from you shortly.

Yours sincerely

Mark

MARK AMBROSE

Summary of day books and petty cash expenditure
Quarter ended 30 September 20X1

Sales day book

	Work done £	VAT £	Total £
July	12,900.00	2,257.50	15,157.50
August	13,200.00	2,310.00	15,510.00
September	12,300.00	2,152.50	14,452.50

Purchase day book

	Net £	VAT £	Total £
July	5,250.00	918.75	6,168.75
August	5,470.00	957.25	6,427.25
September	5,750.00	1,006.25	6,756.25

Petty cash expenditure for quarter (VAT inclusive)

July	£105.75
August	£94.00
September	£117.50

I have also used some materials from my stock, valued at £500 (exclusive of VAT), to repair my garage roof.

Bad debts list – 30 September 20X1

Date	Customer	Total (including VAT)
30 November 20X0	High Melton Farms	£293.75
3 January 20X1	Concorde Motors	£176.25
4 April 20X1	Bawtry Engineering	£117.50

These have now been written off as bad debts.

Task 1

Value Added Tax Return

For the period

01/07/X1 to 30/09/X1

HM Customs
and Excise

Mark Ambrose
High Park House
High Melton
Doncaster
DN5 7EZ

Your VAT Office telephone number is 0151 644211

For Official Use

Registration number	Period
123 9872 17	09 X1

You could be liable to a financial penalty if your completed return and all the VAT payable are not received by the due date.

Due date: 31.10.X1

For official use	

ATTENTION

If you may trade or pay taxes in euro from Jan 1999, Contact your Business Advice Centre for C&E queries or Treasury Enquiry Unit on 020 7270 4558

Before you fill in this form read the notes on the back and the VAT leaflet *'Filling in your VAT Return'*. Fill in all boxes clearly in ink, and write 'none' where necessary. Don't put a dash or leave any box blank. If there are no pence write '**00**' in the pence column. **Do not** enter more than one amount in any box.

			£	p
For official use	VAT due in this period on **sales** and other outputs	1		
	VAT due in this period on **acquisitions** from other **EC Member States**	2		
	Total VAT due (**the sum of boxes 1 and 2**)	3		
	VAT reclaimed in this period on **purchases** and other inputs (including acquisitions from the EC)	4		
	Net VAT to be paid to Customs or reclaimed by you (Difference between boxes 3 and 4)	5		
	Total value of **sales** and all other outputs excluding any VAT. **Include your box 8 figure.**	6		00
	Total value of **purchases** and all other inputs excluding any VAT. **Include your box 9 figure.**	7		00
	Total value of all **supplies** of goods and related services, excl any VAT, to other **EC Member States.**	8		00
	Total value of all **acquisitions** of goods and related servs, excl any VAT, from other **EC Member States.**	9		00

Retail schemes. If you have used any of the schemes in the period covered by this return, enter the relevant letter(s) in this box.

If you are enclosing a payment please tick this box.	DECLARATION: You, or someone on your behalf, must sign below.

I, ...…............ declare that the

(Full name of signatory in BLOCK LETTERS)

information given above is true and complete.

Signature... Date ....20.............

A false declaration can result in prosecution.

VAT 100 (Full)   0141846

PCU (June 1996)

F

Task 2

**DANIEL AND JAMES
LICENSED BOOKKEEPERS**

Stonehill House
Stonehill Rise
Doncaster
DN5 9HB

Tel/Fax: 01302 786050

e-mail: danjames@virgin.net

Partners: James Musgrave
Daniel Robb

_____

_____

_____

QUESTION 90

This scenario based question is divided into three tasks, and contains a large amount of data which you may need to complete the tasks. You are advised to read the whole of the material before commencing the tasks.

You are provided with proforma schedules and report forms for the tasks and these are included at the end of the question.

The situation

Business: Simon White – self-employed bookkeeper

Location: North East Coast of England

You are to adopt the role of Simon White.

Your work includes a bookkeeping and accounting service to small businesses, particularly small hotels and guesthouses, restaurants and public houses.

One of your clients is Crescent Hotel which has 40 bedrooms, a small restaurant and bar. The hotel is owned by John and Norma Thistle. The time is mid October 20X1 and you are currently working on their bookkeeping and VAT records for the quarter ended 30 September 20X1.

Tasks to be completed

Task 1

Immediately following these tasks you will find a summary of the records from the day books for the period ended 30 September, together with other relevant notes.

There is also a short note attached from John Thistle regarding a bad debt.

Using the blank VAT form provided at the end of the question, prepare the return ready for John Thistle's signature.

Task 2

When you have completed the form, John is not around to see you.

Prepare a note for John explaining briefly how you have adjusted the return to account for the matters brought to your attention. Use the space provided at the end of the question for your note.

Task 3

A few days later you receive a phone call from Norma who informs you that she is considering the purchase of a newsagents' shop close to the hotel.

She says that she has heard that special VAT schemes apply to the retail trade.

Before responding fully to her, you decide to write to the VAT office for clarification of the scheme or schemes which apply to this type of business.

Write a letter to the VAT office at:

> Customs House
> Bright Street
> Scarborough
> North Yorkshire YO33 23J

regarding this issue. Use the blank notepaper provided at the end of the question.

Data

CRESCENT HOTEL

Summary of day books for quarter ended 30 September 20X1

Hotel sales day book

	Net £	VAT £	Gross £
July	17,300.00	3,027.50	20,327.50
August	20,200.00	3,535.00	23,735.00
September	17,600.00	3,080.00	20,680.00

Sales - Gross takings in cash

	Bar £	Restaurant £
July	3,877.50	6,873.75
August	4,935.00	6,638.75
September	3,466.25	6,168.75

Purchase day book

		Net £	VAT £	Gross £
July	}	5,190.00	908.25	6,098.25
August	} Hotel	6,060.00	1,060.50	7,120.50
September	}	5,280.00	924.00	6,204.00
July – September (bar and restaurant)		10,800.00	1,890.00	12,690.00

Petty cash expenditure

Gross for period   £481.75

NOTE

To: Simon

From: John

Date: 16 October 20X1

Simon, you are aware that we had three residents last year (December 20X0) from a company working in the area. This company has now gone into liquidation and we have been informed that we will not receive any funds against this debt.

Could you please, if possible, claim back the VAT from Customs and Excise.

The gross value of the invoice was £587.50.

Also, in mid-August it was Norma's birthday and we 'put on' a surprise party for her. We used £300 worth of stock from the restaurant and the bar.

Do we need to adjust any figures for VAT?

KAPLAN PUBLISHING

PROFORMAS FOR ANSWERS

Task 1

Value Added Tax Return	For Official Use
For the period	
01/07/X1 to 30/09/X1	Registration number: 179 6421 27 Period: 09 X1

HM Customs
and Excise

John Thistle
t/as Crescent Hotel
High Street
Whitby
YO21 37L   140784/06

You could be liable to a financial penalty if your completed return and all the VAT payable are not received by the due date.

Due date: 31.10.X1

For official use

Your VAT Office telephone number is 0151 644211

ATTENTION

If you may trade or pay taxes in euro from Jan 1999, Contact your Business Advice Centre for C&E queries or Treasury Enquiry Unit on 020 7270 4558

Before you fill in this form read the notes on the back and the VAT leaflet *'Filling in your VAT Return'*. Fill in all boxes clearly in ink, and write 'none' where necessary. Don't put a dash or leave any box blank. If there are no pence write '00' in the pence column. **Do not** enter more than one amount in any box.

For official use			£	p
	VAT due in this period on **sales** and other outputs	1		
	VAT due in this period on **acquisitions** from other **EC Member States**	2		
	Total VAT due (**the sum of boxes 1 and 2**)	3		
	VAT reclaimed in this period on **purchases** and other inputs (including acquisitions from the EC)	4		
	Net VAT to be paid to Customs or reclaimed by you (Difference between boxes 3 and 4)	5		
	Total value of **sales** and all other outputs excluding any VAT. **Include your box 8 figure.**	6		00
	Total value of **purchases** and all other inputs excluding any VAT. **Include your box 9 figure.**	7		00
	Total value of all **supplies** of goods and related services, excl any VAT, to other **EC Member States.**	8		00
	Total value of all **acquisitions** of goods and related servs, excl any VAT, from other **EC Member States.**	9		00

Retail schemes. If you have used any of the schemes in the period covered by this return, enter the relevant letter(s) in this box.

If you are enclosing a payment please tick this box.	DECLARATION: You, or someone on your behalf, must sign below.

I, ... declare that the
(Full name of signatory in BLOCK LETTERS)
information given above is true and complete.
Signature... Date ....20.............
A false declaration can result in prosecution.

0141846

VAT 100 (Full)   PCU (June 1996)   F

To: John Thistle

From: Simon White

Date: 18 October 20X1

....
....
....
....
....
....
....
....
....
....
....
....
....
....
....
....
....
....
....
....
....
....
....
....
....

KAPLAN PUBLISHING

Task 3

Simon White
Bookkeeper
Bay Farm
High Street
Hawsker
YO21 3EJ

Date: ....

....

....

....

....

....

....

....

....

....

....

....

....

....

....

....

....

....

....

....

....

....

....

Key Technique Answers

Chapter 1
Double entry bookkeeping – introduction

ANSWER 1

(a)   **Opening capital**

		£		£
Assets	Cash	5,000	Capital	5,000

(b)   **Cash purchase**

		£		£
Assets	Stock	500	Capital	5,000
	Cash (5,000 – 500)	4,500		
		5,000		5,000

(c)   **Credit purchase**

		£		£
Assets	Stock (500 + (5 × 200))	1,500	Capital	5,000
	Cash	4,500		
		6,000		
Liabilities	Creditors	(1,000)		
		5,000		5,000

(d)   **Cash sale**

		£		£
Assets	Stock (1,500 – 500)	1,000	Capital	5,000
	Cash (4,500 + 750)	5,250	Profit (750 – 500)	250
		6,250		
Liabilities	Creditors	(1,000)		
		5,250		5,250

(e)   **Cash sale**

		£		£
Assets	Stock (1,000 – 800)	200	Capital	5,000
	Debtors	1,200	Profit (250 + 1,200 – 800)	650
	Cash	5,250		
		6,650		
Liabilities	Creditors	(1,000)		
		5,650		5,650

KAPLAN PUBLISHING

(f)   **Rent payment**

		£		£
Assets	Stock	200	Capital	5,000
	Debtors	1,200	Profit (650 – 250)	400
	Cash (5,250 – 250)	5,000		
		6,400		
Liabilities	Creditors	(1,000)		
		5,400		5,400

(g)   **Drawings**

		£		£
Assets	Stock	200	Capital	5,000
	Debtors	1,200	Profit	400
	Cash (5,000 – 100)	4,900		
		6,300	Drawings	(100)
Liabilities	Creditors	(1,000)		
		5,300		5,300

(h)   **Sundry income**

		£		£
Assets	Stock	200	Capital	5,000
	Debtors (1,200 + 50)	1,250	Profit (400 + 50)	450
	Cash	4,900		
		6,350	Drawings	(100)
Liabilities	Creditors	(1,000)		
		5,350		5,350

(i)   **Payment to creditor**

		£		£
Assets	Stock	200	Capital	5,000
	Debtors	1,250	Profit (450 – 150)	450
	Cash (4,900 – 500)	4,400		
		5,850	Drawings	(100)
Liabilities	Creditors (1,000 – 500)	(500)		
		5,350		5,350

(j)   **Receipt from debtor**

		£		£
Assets	Stock	200	Capital	5,000
	Debtors (1,250 – 1,200)	50	Profit	450
	Cash (4,400 + 1,200)	5,600		
		5,850	Drawings	(100)
Liabilities	Creditors	(500)		
		5,350		5,350

(k)   **Purchase of van**

		£		£
Assets	Van	4,000	Capital	5,000
	Stock	200	Profit	450
				5,450
	Debtors	50		
	Cash (5,600 – 4,000)	1,600	Drawings	(100)
		5,850		
Liabilities	Creditors	(500)		
		5,350		5,350

(l)   **Telephone bill**

		£		£
Assets	Van	4,000	Capital	5,000
	Stock	200	Profit (450 – 150)	300
				5,300
	Debtors	50		
	Cash	1,600	Drawings	(100)
		5,850		
Liabilities	Creditors (500 + 150)	(650)		
		5,200		5,200

ANSWER 2

Accounting equation at 31 January 20X6

		£		£
Assets	Display equipment	50	Capital	3,000
	Stocks of sports equipment (W1)	2,000	Profit (balancing figure)	230
	Debtors	30		
	Cash (W2)	2,500		
		4,580		3,230
Liabilities	Creditors	1,500	Drawings	150
		3,080		3,080

WORKINGS

(1)   **Stock**

	£
Purchased 10 January ($\frac{1}{2} \times$ £1,000)	500
Purchased 31 January	1,500
	2,000

(2)   **Cash**

		£	£
Receipts	Capital paid in		3,000
	From customers		800
			3,800
Payments	Rent	100	
	Suppliers of stock	1,000	
	Suppliers of display equipment	50	
	Drawings	150	
			(1,300)
Balance at 31 January			2,500

Alternative presentation

E Haddock – Accounting equation at 31 January 20X6

	£	£
Fixed assets		
Display equipment		50
Current assets		
Stock	2,000	
Debtors	30	
Cash	2,500	
	4,530	
Current liabilities		
Creditors	1,500	
		3,030
		3,080
Representing		
Capital at 1 January		3,000
Profit for the period (balancing figure)		230
		3,230
Less: Drawings		150
		3,080

Chapter 2
Ledger accounting

ANSWER 3

Bank

	£		£
(a) Capital	4,000	(b) Computer	1,000
(d) Sales	800	(c) Rent	400

Capital

	£		£
		(a) Bank	4,000

Rent

	£		£
(c) Bank	400		

Sales

	£		£
		(d) Bank	800

Computers

	£		£
(b) Bank	1,000		

ANSWER 4

		Debit		Credit	
	Transaction	Account	Reason	Account	Reason
(a)	£4,000 capital	Bank	Cash paid into the bank - an asset	Capital	Cash paid in by owner – a liability
(b)	Computer £1,000	Computer	Increase in assets	Bank	Cash paid out of the bank – a reduction in the value of the asset
(c)	Rent £400	Rent	An expense	Bank	Cash paid out of the bank – a reduction in the value of the asset
(d)	Consultancy £800	Bank	Cash paid into the bank – an asset	Sales	Increase in income

ANSWER 5

Bank

	£		£
(a) Capital	5,000	(b) Purchases	800
(e) Sales	600	(c) Rent	500
(f) Sales	700	(d) Van	2,000
		(g) Purchases	1,000
		(h) Stationery	200
		(i) Drawings	500

Purchases

	£		£
(b) Bank	800		
(g) Bank	1,000		

Capital

	£		£
		(a) Bank	5,000

Rent

	£		£
(c) Bank	500		

Van

	£		£
(d) Bank	2,000		

Sales

	£		£
		(e) Bank	600
		(f) Bank	700

Stationery

	£		£
(h) Bank	200		

Drawings

	£		£
(i) Bank	500		

ANSWER 6

Capital

	£		£
		(a) Bank	4,000

Purchases

	£		£
(b) Bank	700		
(g) Bank	1,200		

Entertainment

	£		£
(c) Bank	300		

Computers

	£		£
(d) Bank	3,000		

Sales

	£		£
		(e) Bank	1,500

Drawings

	£		£
(f) Bank	500		

Telephone

	£		£
(h) Bank	600	(i) Bank	200

Stationery

	£		£
(j) Bank	157		

Bank

	£		£
(a) Capital	4,000	(b) Purchases	700
(e) Sales	1,500	(c) Entertainment	300
(i) Telephone	200	(d) Computers	3,000
		(f) Drawings	500
		(g) Purchases	1,200
		(h) Telephone	600
		(j) Stationery	157

ANSWER 7

Capital

	£		£
		(a) Bank	2,000

Purchases

	£		£
(b) Bank	1,000		
(f) Bank	1,000		

Van

	£		£
(c) Bank	900		

Sales

	£		£
		(d) Bank	2,500

Consultancy services

	£		£
		(e) Bank	3,000

Stationery

	£		£
(g) Bank	260	(j) Bank	100

Rent

	£		£
(h) Bank	750		

Wages

	£		£
(i) Bank	600		

Bank

	£		£
(a) Capital	2,000	(b) Purchases	1,000
(d) Sales	2,500	(c) Van	900
(e) Consultancy	3,000	(f) Purchases	1,000
(j) Stationery	100	(g) Stationery	260
		(h) Rent	750
		(i) Wages	600

ANSWER 8

Sales

	£		£
		B	1,000
		C	90

B

	£		£
Sales	1,000	Bank	500

C

	£		£
Sales	90	Bank	90

Bank

	£		£
B	500		
C	90		

ANSWER 9

Purchases

	£		£
Y	600		
Z	750		

Y

	£		£
Bank	300	Purchases	600

Z

	£		£
Bank	500	Purchases	750

Bank

	£		£
		Y	300
		Z	500

KAPLAN PUBLISHING

Chapter 3
Balancing the ledger accounts

ANSWER 10

Bank

	£		£
Capital	10,000	Computer	1,000
Sales	2,000	Telephone	567
Sales	3,000	Rent	1,500
Sales	2,000	Rates	125
		Stationery	247
		Petrol	49
		Purchases	2,500
		Drawings	500
		Petrol	42
		Balance c/d	10,470
	17,000		17,000
Balance b/d	10,470		

ANSWER 11

Bank

	£		£
Capital	5,000	Purchases	850
Sales	1,000	Fixtures	560
Sales	876	Van	1,500
Rent rebate	560	Rent	1,300
Sales	1,370	Rates	360
		Telephone	220
		Stationery	120
		Petrol	48
		Car repairs	167
		Balance c/d	3,681
	8,806		8,806
Balance b/d	3,681		

ANSWER 12

Bank

	£		£
Balance b/f	23,700	Drawings	4,000
Sales	2,300	Rent	570
Sales	1,700	Purchases	6,000
Debtors	4,700	Rates	500
		Salaries	3,600
		Car expenses	460
		Petrol	49
		Petrol	38
		Electricity	210
		Stationery	89
		Balance c/d	16,884
	32,400		32,400
Balance b/d	16,884		

ANSWER 13

	North	South	East	West	Total
Garden plants	253,865	27,598	315,634	109,521	706,618
Garden equipment	2,734,384	274,393	382,726	3,726,125	7,117,628
Consultancy	2,438,549	374,385	3,728,398	37,261	6,578,593
TOTAL	5,426,798	676,376	4,426,758	3,872,907	14,402,839

ANSWER 14

Date	Narrative	Folio	Total	Creditors	Stationery	Rent	Telephone	Postage	Fixed assets	Sundry
			35,800	23,894	678	4,563	5,675	456	456	78
			62,643	6,743					55,433	467
			58,547	56,432	654	675				786
			8,421	5,643	564		786	78	564	786
			11,147	675	89			675	765	8,943
			9,287	6,754	675		785	78	897	98
TOTAL			185,845	100,141	2,660	5,238	7,246	1,287	58,115	11,158

KAPLAN PUBLISHING

Chapter 4
Credit sales – discounts and VAT

ANSWER 15

(a) VAT = £140.00 × 17.5% = £24.50

(b) VAT = £560.00 × 17.5% = £98.00

(c) VAT = $£780.00 \times \dfrac{17.5}{117.5}$ = £116.17

(d) VAT = $£970.00 \times \dfrac{17.5}{117.5}$ = £144.47

ANSWER 16

(a) VAT = £(280 – (2% × 280)) × 17.5% = £48.02

(b) VAT = £(480 – (3% × 480)) × 17.5% = £81.48

(c) VAT = £(800 – (5% × 800)) × 17.5% = £133.00

(d) VAT = £(650 – (4% × 650)) × 17.5% = £109.20

ANSWER 17

(a)   B takes the settlement discount:

	£
Net price	600.00
VAT £(600 – (3% × 600)) × 17.5%	101.85
Invoice value	701.85

Amount paid by B:

	£
Invoice value	701.85
Less: 3% × 600	(18.00)
Amount paid	683.85

(b)   B does not take the settlement discount:

	£
Net price	600.00
VAT £(600 – (3% × 600)) × 17.5%	101.85
Invoice value	701.85

If B does not take the settlement discount, B will pay the full £701.85.

ANSWER 18

(a)   C takes the settlement discount:

	£
Net price	700.00
VAT £(700 – (5% × 700)) × 17.5%	116.37
Invoice value	816.37
Less: 5% discount = 700 × 5%	(35.00)
Amount paid by C	781.37

Sales

	£		£
		SLCA	700.00

SLCA

	£		£
Sales + VAT	816.37	Bank	781.37
		Discount allowed	35.00
	816.37		816.37

Bank

	£		£
SLCA	781.37		

VAT

	£		£
		SLCA	116.37

Discount allowed

	£		£
SLCA	35.00		

(b)   C does not take the settlement discount:

	£
Invoice value (per (a))	816.37

As C does not take the settlement discount, he pays the full amount (£816.37).

Sales

	£		£
		SLCA	700.00

SLCA

	£		£
Sales + VAT	816.37	Bank	816.37

Bank

	£		£
SLCA	816.37		

VAT

	£		£
		SLCA	116.37

Chapter 5
The sales day book – main and subsidiary ledgers

ANSWER 19

Sales day book

Date	Invoice No	Customer name	Code	Total £	VAT £	Net £
20X1						
1/5	03466	Fraser & Co	SL14	151.19	22.51	128.68
	03467	Letterhead Ltd	SL03	303.03	45.13	257.90
2/5	03468	Jeliteen Traders	SL15	113.48	16.90	96.58
	CN0746	Garner & Co	SL12	(80.72)	(12.02)	(68.70)
3/5	03469	Harper Bros	SL22	315.07	46.92	268.15
	03470	Juniper Ltd	SL17	123.82	18.44	105.38
4/5	03471	H G Frank	SL30	346.23	51.56	294.67
	CN0747	Hill Traders	SL26	(138.27)	(20.59)	(117.68)
5/5	03472	Keller Assocs	SL07	129.93	19.35	110.58
				1,263.76	188.20	1,075.56

ANSWER 20

Sales day book

Date	Invoice No	Customer name	Code	Total £	VAT £	01 £	02 £	03 £	04 £
18/4/X1	06116	B Z S Music	SL01	1,426.15	206.95		432.00		787.20
18/4/X1	06117	M T Retail	SL29	628.62	93.62	210.00			325.00
18/4/X1	06118	Harmer & Co	SL17	1,016.51	147.51		575.00	294.00	
				3,071.28	448.08	210.00	1,007.00	294.00	1,112.20

Note that when a trade discount has been deducted on the invoice in total it must be deducted from each type of sale when entering the figures in the analysed sales day book.

ANSWER 21

Sales day book

Date	Invoice No	Customer name	Code	Total £	VAT £	Maintenance £	Decorating £
01/5/X1	07891	Portman & Co	P2	162.83	23.83	139.00	
03/5/X1	07892	Stanton Assocs	S3	1,288.65	188.65		1,100.00
05/5/X1	07893	Boreham Bros	B7	277.30	41.30	106.00	130.00
				1,728.78	253.78	245.00	1,230.00

ANSWER 22

Sales day book							
Date	Invoice No	Customer name	Code	Total	VAT	Group 01	Group 02
				£	£	£	£
20X0							
1 Feb	61612	Worker Ltd	SL11	217.37	32.37	68.90	116.10
4 Feb	61613	P T Assocs	SL04	122.38	18.22		104.16
5 Feb	61614	Paul Bros	SL13	289.27	43.08	106.19	140.00
8 Feb	61615	S D Partners	SL07	109.54	16.31	72.40	20.83
9 Feb	61616	Harper Ltd	SL08	399.97	59.57	160.18	180.22
11 Feb	C241	P T Assocs	SL04	(23.68)	(3.52)		(20.16)
15 Feb	61617	Worker Ltd	SL11	144.26	21.48	50.60	72.18
17 Feb	61618	P T Assocs	SL04	201.67	30.03	60.41	111.23
18 Feb	61619	Harper Ltd	SL08	345.15	51.40	110.15	183.60
22 Feb	C242	Paul Bros	SL13	(35.72)	(5.32)	(10.18)	(20.22)
25 Feb	61620	P T Assocs	SL04	129.01	19.21	62.17	47.63
26 Feb	61621	S D Partners	SL07	56.58	8.42	48.16	
				1,955.80	291.25	728.98	935.57

Main ledger accounts

Sales ledger control account

		£		£
28/2	SDB	1,955.80		

Sales account – 01

	£			£
		28/2 SDB		728.98

Sales account – 02

	£			£
		28/2 SDB		935.57

VAT account

	£			£
		28/2 SDB		291.25

Subsidiary ledger accounts

Worker Ltd   SL11

		£		£
1/2	SDB 61612	217.37		
15/2	SDB 61617	144.26		

P T Assocs   SL04

		£			£
4/2	SDB 61613	122.38	11/2	SDB C241	23.68
17/2	SDB 61618	201.67			
25/2	SDB 61620	129.01			

Paul Bros   SL13

		£			£
5/2	SDB 61614	289.27	22/2	SDB C242	35.72

S D Partners   SL07

		£			£
8/2	SDB 61615	109.54			
26/2	SDB 61621	56.58			

Harper Ltd   SL08

		£			£
9/2	SDB 61616	399.97			
18/2	SDB 61619	345.15			

ANSWER 23

Main ledger accounts

Sales ledger control account

		£			£
			30/4	SRDB	140.19

Sales returns – 01

		£		£
30/4	SRDB	54.01		

Sales returns – 02

		£		£
30/4	SRDB	32.06		

Sales returns – 03

		£		£
30/4	SRDB	33.25		

VAT account

		£		£
30/4	SRDB	20.87		

Subsidiary ledger accounts

Gerard & Co   G01

		£			£
			7/4	SRDB 2114	34.36

	Filmer Ltd			F02
£				£
	15/4	SRDB 2115		44.92

	T Harrison			H04
£				£
	20/4	SRDB 2116		24.44

	Rolls Ltd			R01
£				£
	28/4	SRDB 2117		36.47

Chapter 6
The analysed cash receipts book

ANSWER 24

(a)   **Cash receipts book**

Date	Narrative	SL Code	Total	VAT	Debtors	Cash sales	Discount
			£	£	£	£	£
20X1							
28/4	G Heilbron	SL04	108.45		108.45		
	L Tessa	SL15	110.57		110.57		3.31
	J Dent	SL17	210.98		210.98		6.32
	F Trainer	SL21	97.60		97.60		
	A Winter	SL09	105.60		105.60		3.16
	Cash sales		265.08	39.48		225.60	
			898.28	39.48	633.20	225.60	12.79

(b)   **Main ledger**

VAT account

					£
£					
	28/4	CRB			39.48

Sales ledger control account

£					£
	28/4	CRB			633.20
		CRB – discount			12.79

Sales account

£					£
	28/4	CRB			225.60

Discount allowed account

		£			£
28/4	CRB	12.79			

(c)   **Subsidiary ledger**

		G Heilbron		**SL04**
	£			£
		28/4	CRB	108.45

		L Tessa		**SL15**
	£			£
		28/4	CRB	110.57
			CRB – discount	3.31

		J Dent		**SL17**
	£			£
		28/4	CRB	210.98
			CRB – discount	6.32

		F Trainer		**SL21**
	£			£
		28/4	CRB	97.60

		A Winter		**SL09**
	£			£
		28/4	CRB	105.60
			CRB – discount	3.16

ANSWER 25

(a)   **Cash receipts book**

Date	Narrative	SL Code	Total £	VAT £	Debtors £	Cash sales £	Discount £
20X1							
15/5	McCaul & Partners	M04	147.56		147.56		2.95
	Dunn Assocs	D02	264.08		264.08		
	P Martin	M02	167.45		167.45		
	F Little	L03	265.89		265.89		7.97
	D Raine	R01	158.02		158.02		3.95
	Cash sales		446.50	66.50		380.00	
			1,449.50	66.50	1,003.00	380.00	14.87

(Note that the total of the 'Discount' column is not included in the cross-cast total of £1,449.50. The discounts allowed are entered into the cash receipts book on a memorandum basis; the total at the end of each period is posted to the sales ledger control account and to an expense account.)

(b)   Main ledger

VAT account

	£				£
		15/5	CRB		66.50

Sales ledger control account

	£				£
		15/5	CRB		1,003.00
		15/5	CRB – discount		14.87

Sales account

	£				£
		15/5	CRB		380.00

Discount allowed

		£		£
15/5	CRB	14.87		

(c)   Subsidiary ledger

McCaul & Partners

	£				£
		15/5	CRB		147.56
		15/5	CRB – discount		2.95

Dunn Associates

	£				£
		15/5	CRB		264.08

P Martin

	£				£
		15/5	CRB		167.45

F Little

	£				£
		15/5	CRB		265.89
		15/5	CRB – discount		7.97

D Raine

	£				£
		15/5	CRB		158.02
		15/5	CRB – discount		3.95

Chapter 7
Credit purchases – discounts and VAT

ANSWER 26

(a) VAT = £400 × 17.5% = £70.00

(b) VAT = £650 × 17.5% = £113.75

(c) VAT = $£425 \times \dfrac{17.5}{117.5}$ = £63.29

(d) VAT = $£77 \times \dfrac{17.5}{117.5}$ = £11.46

ANSWER 27

(a) VAT = £(850 – (3% × 850)) × 17.5% = £144.28

(b) VAT = £(600 – (5% × 600)) × 17.5% = £99.75

(c) VAT = £(325 – (2% × 325)) × 17.5% = £55.73

(d) VAT = £(57 – (4% × 57)) × 17.5% = £9.57

ANSWER 28

Calculate the invoice value and amount paid by Z.

	£
Net price	600.00
VAT £(600 – (3% × 600)) × 17.5%	101.85
Invoice value	701.85
Less: Discount 3% × 600	(18.00)
Amount paid	683.85

Purchases

	£		£
PLCA	600.00		

PLCA

	£		£
Bank	683.85	Purchases + VAT	701.85
Discount	18.00		
	701.85		701.85

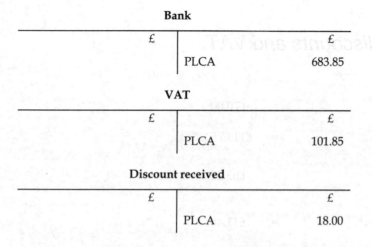

Bank

£		£
	PLCA	683.85

VAT

£		£
	PLCA	101.85

Discount received

£		£
	PLCA	18.00

Chapter 8
The purchases day book – main and subsidiary ledgers

ANSWER 29

Purchases day book

Date	Invoice no	Code	Supplier	Total	VAT	Fabric	Header tape	Other
12/4/X1	06738	PL03	Fabric Supplies Ltd	1,097.22	160.62	798.00	138.60	
	0328	PL04	Lillian Fisher	107.74	16.04			91.70
	CN0477	PL05	Headstream & Co	(79.90)	(11.90)	(51.40)	(16.60)	
	07359	PL01	Mainstream Fabrics	330.04	48.52	281.52		
				1,455.10	213.28	1,028.12	122.00	91.70

ANSWER 30

Purchases day book

Date	Invoice no	Code	Supplier	Total	VAT	Wood	Bricks/ cement	Consumables
3/5/X1	077401	PL16	Magnum Supplies	493.90	72.30		421.60	
	046193	PL08	A J Broom & Co Ltd	118.47	17.64	85.08		15.75
	47823	PL13	Jenson Ltd	433.74	62.94	284.80	86.00	
				1,046.11	152.88	369.88	507.60	15.75

ANSWER 31

Purchases returns day book

Date	Credit note no	Code	Supplier	Total	VAT	Wood	Bricks/ cement	Consumables
3/5/X1	CN06113	PL13	Jenson Ltd	30.07	4.36	25.71		
	06132	PL03	Haddow Bros	41.70	6.10	35.60		
	C4163	PL16	Magnum Supplies	45.80	6.70		39.10	
				117.57	17.16	61.31	39.10	-

ANSWER 32

Main ledger

Purchases ledger control account

		£			£
19/4	PRDB	245.10	12/4	Balance b/f	12,678.57

VAT account

		£			£
			12/4	Balance b/f	1,023.90
			19/4	PRDB	36.50

Purchases returns – 01 account

		£			£
			12/4	Balance b/f	337.60
			19/4	PRDB	60.40

Purchases returns – 02 account

		£			£
			12/4	Balance b/f	228.59
			19/4	PRDB	23.40

Purchases returns – 03 account

		£			£
			12/4	Balance b/f	889.46
			19/4	PRDB	108.00

Purchases returns – 04 account

		£			£
			12/4	Balance b/f	362.78
			19/4	PRDB	16.80

Subsidiary ledger

<table>
<tr><td></td><td></td><td>£</td><td colspan="2" align="right">F Williams</td><td>PL06</td></tr>
</table>

		£			£
18/4	PRDB C4772	164.50	12/4	Balance b/f	673.47

K Bartlett — PL13

		£			£
19/4	PRDB 06638	53.11	12/4	Balance b/f	421.36

J D Withers — PL16

		£			£
15/4	PRDB C0179	27.49	12/4	Balance b/f	446.37

ANSWER 33

Main ledger

Purchases ledger control account

		£			£
			1 May	Balance b/d	3,104.67
			5 May	PDB	1,002.57

VAT account

		£			£
5 May	PDB	149.30	1 May	Balance b/d	723.56

Purchases account

		£		£
1 May	Balance b/d	24,367.48		
5 May	PDB	853.27		

Subsidiary ledger

T Ives — PL01

		£			£
			1 May	Balance b/d	332.56
			5 May	PDB 002633	192.98

H Samuels — PL02

		£			£
			1 May	Balance b/d	286.90
			3 May	PDB 92544	109.79

L Jameson

PL03

			£				£
				1 May	Balance b/d		623.89
				1 May	PDB 36558		393.91

G Rails

PL04

			£				£
				1 May	Balance b/d		68.97
				4 May	PDB 03542		180.93

K Davison

PL07

			£				£
				1 May	Balance b/d		125.47
				1 May	PDB 102785		124.96

Chapter 9
The analysed cash payments book

ANSWER 34

Cash payments book

Date	Details	Cheque no	Code	Total £	VAT £	Purchases ledger £	Cash purchases £	Other £	Discounts received £
12/3/X1	Homer Ltd	03648	PL12	168.70		168.70			5.06
	Forker & Co	03649	PL07	179.45		179.45			5.38
	Purchases	03650		334.87	49.87		285.00		
	Print Ass.	03651	PL08	190.45		190.45			
	ABG Ltd	03652	PL02	220.67		220.67			6.62
	Purchases	03653		193.87	28.87		165.00		
	G Greg	03654	PL19	67.89		67.89			
				1,355.90	78.74	827.16	450.00	-	17.06

Main ledger

Purchases ledger control account

		£			£
12/3	CPB	827.16	5/3	Balance b/d	4,136.24
12/3	CPB – discount	17.06			

VAT account

		£			£
12/3	CPB	78.74	5/3	Balance b/d	1,372.56

Purchases account

		£			£
5/3	Balance b/d	20,465.88			
12/3	CPB	450.00			

Discounts received account

		£			£
			5/3	Balance b/d	784.56
			12/3	CPB	17.06

Subsidiary ledger

ABG Ltd — PL02

		£			£
12/3	CPB 03652	220.67	5/3	Balance b/d	486.90
12/3	CPB – discount	6.62			

Forker & Co — PL07

		£			£
12/3	CPB 03649	179.45	5/3	Balance b/d	503.78
12/3	CPB – discount	5.38			

Print Associates — PL08

		£			£
12/3	CPB 03651	190.45	5/3	Balance b/d	229.56

Homer Ltd — PL12

		£			£
12/3	CPB 03648	168.70	5/3	Balance b/d	734.90
12/3	CPB – discount	5.06			

G Greg — PL19

		£			£
12/3	CPB 03654	67.89	5/3	Balance b/d	67.89

ANSWER 35

Cash payments book

Date	Details	Cheque no	Code	Total £	VAT £	Purchases ledger £	Cash purchases £	Other £	Discounts received £
20X1									
30/5	J M Bond	200572	PL01	247.56		247.56			
	Magnum Supplies	200573	PL16	662.36		662.36			13.25
	A J Broom	200574	PL08	153.57		153.57			
	Jenson Ltd	200575	PL13	336.57		336.57			6.73
	KKL Traders	200576	PL20	442.78		442.78			8.85
	Purchases	200577		108.66	16.18		92.48		
				1,951.50	16.18	1,842.84	92.48	-	28.83

Main ledger

Purchases ledger control account

	£			£
30 May CPB	1,842.84	23 May	Balance b/d	5,328.46
30 May CPB – discount	28.83			

VAT account

	£			£
30 May CPB	16.18	23 May	Balance b/d	1,365.35

Purchases account

	£		£
23 May Balance b/d	36,785.90		
30 May CPB	92.48		

Discount received account

	£			£
		23 May	Balance b/d	1,573.56
		30 May	CPB	28.83

Subsidiary ledger

J M Bond   PL01

	£			£
30 May CPB 200572	247.56	23 May	Balance b/d	247.56

A J Broom Ltd   PL08

		£				£
30 May	CPB 200574	153.57	23 May	Balance b/d		524.36

Jenson Ltd   PL13

		£				£
30 May	CPB 200575	336.57	23 May	Balance b/d		512.36
30 May	CPB – discount	6.73				

Magnum Supplies   PL16

		£				£
30 May	CPB 200573	662.36	23 May	Balance b/d		675.61
30 May	CPB – discount	13.25				

KKL Traders   PL20

		£				£
30 May	CPB 200576	442.78	23 May	Balance b/d		612.46
30 May	CPB – discount	8.85				

Chapter 10
Credit sales: documents

ANSWER 36

CREDIT NOTE

Credit Note to:	**Keyboard Supplies**
H M Music	Trench Park Estate
Tenant House	Fieldham
Perley TN7 8ER	Sussex TN21 4AF
	Tel: 01829 654545
	Fax: 01829 654646

Credit Note no:	CN0337
Tax point:	17 April 20X1
VAT reg no:	466 1128 30
Your reference:	SL09
Purchase order no:	

Code	Description	Quantity	VAT rate %	Unit price £	Amount exclusive of VAT £
B3060	Bento Keyboard	1	17.5	126.00	126.00

	126.00
Trade discount 15%	18.90
	107.10
VAT at 17.5%	18.74
Total amount	125.84

ANSWER 37

INVOICE

Invoice to:
Musicolor Ltd
23 High Street
Nutford
Sussex TN11 4TZ

Keyboard Supplies
Trench Park Estate
Fieldham
Sussex TN21 4AF
Tel: 01829 654545
Fax: 01829 654646

Deliver to:

As above

Invoice no:	06113
Tax point:	17 April 20X1
VAT reg no:	466 1128 30
Your reference:	SL06
Purchase order no:	04 318

Code	Description	Quantity	VAT rate %	Unit price £	Amount exclusive of VAT £
Z4600	Zanni Keyboard	2	17.5	185.00	370.00
A4802	Atol Keyboard	3	17.5	130.00	390.00
					760.00
Trade discount 10%					76.00
					684.00
VAT at 17.5%					116.10
Total amount payable					800.10

Deduct discount of 3% if paid within 10 days, 30 days net

INVOICE

Invoice to:
Newford Music
32/34 Main Street
Welland
Sussex TN4 6BD

Keyboard Supplies
Trench Park Estate
Fieldham
Sussex TN21 4AF
Tel: 01829 654545
Fax: 01829 654646

Deliver to:

As above

Invoice no:	06114
Tax point:	17 April 20X1
VAT reg no:	466 1128 30
Your reference:	SL18
Purchase order no:	47115

Code	Description	Quantity	VAT rate %	Unit price £	Amount exclusive of VAT £
Z4406	Zanni Keyboard	4	17.5	165.00	660.00
					660.00
Trade discount 20%					132.00
					528.00
VAT at 17.5%					89.62
Total amount payable					617.62

Deduct discount of 3% if paid within 10 days, 30 days net

INVOICE

Invoice to:
F T Music Supplies
The Barn
Nutford
Sussex TN11 7AJ

Keyboard Supplies
Trench Park Estate
Fieldham
Sussex TN21 4AF
Tel: 01829 654545
Fax: 01829 654646

Deliver to:

As above

Invoice no:	06115
Tax point:	17 April 20X1
VAT reg no:	466 1128 30
Your reference:	SL23
Purchase order no:	71143

Code	Description	Quantity	VAT rate %	Unit price £	Amount exclusive of VAT £
B2010	Bento Keyboard	2	17.5	148.00	296.00
G4706	Garland Keyboard	3	17.5	96.00	288.00

	584.00
Trade discount 15%	87.60
	496.40
VAT at 17.5%	86.87
Total amount payable	583.27

Chapter 11

Debtors' statements

ANSWER 38

FARMHOUSE
PICKLES
LTD

225 School Lane
Weymouth
Dorset   WE36 5NR
Tel: 0261 480444
Fax: 0261 480555
Date: 30 April 20X1

To: Grant & Co

STATEMENT

Date	Transaction	Debit £	Credit £	Balance £
1 April	Opening balance			337.69
4 April	Inv 32656	150.58		488.27
12 April	Credit 0335		38.70	449.57
18 April	Inv 32671	179.52		629.09
20 April	Payment Discount		330.94	
	Credit 0346		6.75	291.40
24 April	Inv 32689		17.65	273.75
25 April		94.36		368.11

May we remind you that our credit terms are 30 days

FARMHOUSE
PICKLES
LTD

225 School Lane
Weymouth
Dorset   WE36 5NR
Tel: 0261 480444
Fax: 0261 480555
Date: 30 April 20X1

To: Mitchell Partners

STATEMENT

Date	Transaction	Debit £	Credit £	Balance £
1 April	Opening balance			180.46
7 April	Inv 32662	441.57		622.03
12 April	Credit 0344		66.89	555.14
20 April	Inv 32669	274.57		829.71
21 April	Payment Discount		613.58	
			8.45	207.68

May we remind you that our credit terms are 30 days

ANSWER 39

Task 1   No errors noted in journal entry form.

Task 2 and Task 6

MAIN LEDGER

Account name   <u>Sales ledger control</u>   Account no   <u>01 06 10 00</u>

23/11/X1	b/f		3,705.63	27/11/X1	Cash	118.08
30/11/X1	Journal 3347	21,018.39		29/11/X1	Cash	118.08
				30/11/X1	Journal 3348	466.18

Account name   <u>Sales - Product 01</u>   Account no   <u>03 70 10 01</u>

		23/11/X1	b/f	34,875.94
		30/11/X1	Journal 3347	1,395.78

Account name   <u>Sales - Product 02</u>   Account no   <u>03 70 10 02</u>

		23/11/X1	b/f	175,311.50
		30/11/X1	Journal 3347	7,666.82

Account name   <u>Sales - Product 03</u>   Account no   <u>03 70 10 03</u>

		23/11/X1	b/f	123,844.73
		30/11/X1	Journal 3347	5,557.46

MAIN LEDGER

Account name   Sales - Product 04   Account no   03 70 10 04

		23/11/X1 b/f	78,914.90
		30/11/X1 Journal 3347	3,267.93

Account name   VAT control   Account no   02 08 90 00

30/11/X1 Journal 3348	69.42	23/11/X1 b/f	20,935.86
		30/11/X1 Journal 3347	3,130.40

Account name   Sales returns - Product 01   Account no   04 60 10 01

23/11/X1 b/f	3,105.89		

Account name   Sales returns - Product 02   Account no   04 60 10 02

23/11/X1 b/f	15,222.75		
30/11/X1 Journal 3348	111.16		

Account name   Sales returns - Product 03   Account no   04 60 10 03

23/11/X1 b/f	10,413.67		
30/11/X1 Journal 3348	123.80		

KAPLAN PUBLISHING

MAIN LEDGER

Account name   <u>Sales returns - Product 04</u>   Account no   <u>04 60 10 04</u>

23/11/X1	b/f	6,116.70
30/11/X1	Journal 3348	161.80

Task 3 and Task 7

SUBSIDIARY (SALES) LEDGER ACCOUNTS

Customer name   Arnold Toys   Account number   A2
Customer address   57 Gray Street Bath BA1 2NT
Telephone   01225 633112
Dr   Cr

Date	Transaction	£		Date	Transaction	£	
19/11	Invoice 2195	118	08	20/11	CR 2198	323	60
20/11	Invoice 2198	2,201	95		c/f	1,996	43
		2,320	03			2,320	03
23/11	b/f	1,996	43	27/11	Cash	118	08
27/11	Invoice 2208	456	19	29/11	Cash	118	08

Customer name   Gerald Blythe & Sons   Account number   B2
Customer address   121 St John's Road Cambridge CB2 3AH
Telephone   01223 461922
Dr   Cr

Date	Transaction	£		Date	Transaction	£	
12/11	Invoice 2186	325	11	20/11	Cash	325	11
22/11	Invoice 2203	119	80		c/f	119	80
		444	91			444	91
23/11	b/f	119	80				
30/11	Invoice 2214	629	68	26/11	CN C461	190	11

SUBSIDIARY (SALES) LEDGER ACCOUNTS

Customer name   Daisychains   Account number   D2
Customer address   111 George Street Crawley RH10 1HL
Telephone   01293 811566
Dr   Cr

Date	Transaction	£		Date	Transaction	£	
13/9	Invoice 2103	3,115	11				
27/9	Invoice 2122	211	55		c/f	3,326	66
		3,326	66			3,326	66
28/9	b/f	3,326	66	19/10	Cash	3,115	11
16/10	Invoice 2150	501	30		c/f	712	85
		3,827	96			3,827	96
19/10	b/f	712	85				
23/10	Invoice 2157	871	07		c/f	1,583	92
		1,583	92			1,583	92
26/10	b/f	1,583	92				
26/11	Invoice 2205	1,661	63				
28/11	Invoice 2211	2,057	17				

Customer name   Gameboard Ltd   Account number   G4
Customer address   15 Park Street Woking GU21 1BY
Telephone   01483 757442
Dr   Cr

Date	Transaction	£		Date	Transaction	£	
2/11	b/f	3	09	8/11	Cr	3	09
14/11	Invoice 2187	115	83	16/11	CONTRA	86	94
					c/f	28	89
		115	83			115	83
16/11	b/f	28	89	20/11	Cash	28	89
29/11	Invoice 2212	2,657	24				

SUBSIDIARY (SALES) LEDGER ACCOUNTS

Customer name   Highlight Ltd   Account number   H3

Customer address   10 Station Road St Albans AL4 3EH

Telephone   01727 46737

Dr   Cr

Date	Transaction	£		Date	Transaction	£	
2/11	Invoice 2173	202	95	14/9	b/f	33	75
					c/f	169	20
		202	95			202	95
2/11	b/f	169	20	16/11	Cash	169	20
14/11	Invoice 2185	311	87		c/f	311	87
		481	07			481	07
16/11	b/f	311	87	22/11	Cash	311	87
27/11	Invoice 2209	260	98	30/11	CN C462	47	70

Customer name   Jubilee Games & Toys   Account number   J2

Customer address   3 Bourne Avenue Bracknell RG12 1AR

Telephone   01344 678222

Dr   Cr

Date	Transaction	£		Date	Transaction	£	
23/10	Invoice 2159	86	90	13/11	Cash	73	20
26/11	Invoice 2206	4,325	30				

SUBSIDIARY (SALES) LEDGER ACCOUNTS

Customer name   Lighthouse Products   Account number   L1
Customer address   135 Chapel Road Windsor S14 1UL
Telephone   01753 828688
Dr   Cr

Date	Transaction	£		Date	Transaction	£	
13/11	Invoice 2188	326	11	20/11	CONTRA	44	22
	c/f	44	22	21/11	Cash	326	11
		370	33			370	33
28/11	Invoice 2210	7,069	34	23/11	b/f	44	22
				30/11	CN C463	228	37

Customer name   Mirabelle Leisure   Account number   M3
Customer address   19 Masons Hill Brighton BN1 8RT
Telephone   01273 207146
Dr   Cr

Date	Transaction	£		Date	Transaction	£	
14/11	Invoice 2189	411	38				
15/11	Invoice 2190	83	91		c/f	495	29
		495	29			495	29
16/11	b/f	495	29	20/11	Cash	459	29
					c/f	36	00
		495	29			495	29
23/11	b/f	36	00				
27/11	Invoice 2207	954	04				
29/11	Invoice 2213	946	82				

Task 4

Date	Code	Customer	CN	Total	01	02	03	04	VAT
Sales returns day book									
				£	£	£	£	£	£
26/11/X1	B2	Gerald Blythe	C461	190.11				161.80	28.31
30/11/X1	H3	Highlight Ltd	C462	47.70			40.60		7.10
30/11/X1	L1	Lighthouse Products	C463	228.37		111.16	83.20		34.01
				466.18	–	111.16	123.80	161.80	69.42

Task 5

JOURNAL SALES RETURNS DAY BOOK POSTINGS		NO 3348
Prepared by	*Week ending*	30/11/X1
Authorised by		

Account	Debit	Credit
Sales ledger control		466.18
Sales returns product 01	–	
Sales returns product 02	111.16	
Sales returns product 03	123.80	
Sales returns product 04	161.80	
VAT	69.42	
TOTALS	466.18	466.18

Task 8

TOYBOX GAMES LTD

125 Finchley Way Bristol BS1 4PL Tel: 01272 200299

STATEMENT OF ACCOUNT

Customer name	Daisychains	Customer account no				D2	
Customer address	111 George Street Crawley RH10 1HL						

Statement date	30/11/X1	Dr		Cr		Balance	
Date	**Transaction**	**£**	**p**	**£**	**p**	**£**	**p**
31/10/X1	Balance brought forward	1,583	92			1,583	92
26/11/X1	Invoice 2205	1,661	63			3,245	55
28/11/X1	Invoice 2211	2,057	17			5,302	72
						5,302	72

TOYBOX GAMES LTD

125 Finchley Way Bristol BS1 4PL Tel: 01272 200299

STATEMENT OF ACCOUNT

Customer name	Jubilee Games & Toys	Customer account no				J2	
Customer address	3 Bourne Avenue Bracknell RG12 1AR						

Statement date	30/11/X1	Dr		Cr		Balance	
Date	**Transaction**	**£**	**p**	**£**	**p**	**£**	**p**
31/10/X1	Balance brought forward	86	90			86	90
13/11/X1	Cash			73	20	13	70
26/11/X1	Invoice 2206	4,325	30			4,339	00
						4,339	00

ANSWER 40

Task 1   Sales invoices

39117	missing
39118	clerical error on Peters' total
39120	discount omitted

The corrected invoices are shown on the pages which follow.

SALES INVOICE

ELLIOTT BROOK ASSOCIATES

39118

Address

25 Eaton Terrace		Telephone	01323 866755
Eastbourne BN16 3RS		Fax	01323 995655
VAT Reg No	**544 2900 17**	**Tax point**	**16 May 20X0**

Hire of staff

FAO The Manager
Kenmare Hotel
73 East Sands Way
Eastbourne

Client code KEN 11

Name	Start	Finish	Hours	Grade	Rate £	Total excl VAT £
Price	10/5/X0	13/5/X0	12	D	3.00	36.00
Haines	11/5/X0	13/5/X0	16	C	4.00	64.00
Peters	7/5/X0	12/5/X0	30	B	6.25	187.50
						287.50
			Discount			0
						287.50
			VAT at 17.5%			50.31
						337.81 : £337.81

SALES INVOICE						

ELLIOTT BROOK ASSOCIATES

39120

Address

25 Eaton Terrace		Telephone	01323 866755
Eastbourne BN16 3RS		Fax	01323 995655
VAT Reg No	**544 2900 17**	**Tax point**	**16 May 20X0**

Hire of staff

FAO Services Manager
Royal Hotel
Royal View
Eastbourne

Client code ROY 05

Name	Start	Finish	Hours	Grade	Rate £	Total excl VAT £
Clarke	7/5/X0	8/5/X0	15	A	7.50	112.50
Hartley	9/5/X0	13/5/X0	40	A	7.50	300.00
						412.50
			Discount			41.25
						371.25
			VAT at 17.5%			64.97
						436.22 : £436.22

Task 2

SALES DAY BOOK					
DATE	CLIENT	INVOICE	NET £	VAT £	GROSS £
16/5/X0	IMPERIAL	39114	270.00	47.25	317.25
	ROSETREE	39115	196.75	34.43	231.18
	WEST BAY	39116	179.25	31.37	210.62
		39117			
	KENMARE	39118	287.50	50.31	337.81
	SEAVIEW	39119	180.00	31.50	211.50
	ROYAL HOTEL	39120	371.25	64.97	436.22
	CROWN AND ANCHOR	39121	30.00	5.25	35.25
16/5/X0	TOTAL		1,514.75	265.08	1,779.83

Task 3   Credit notes

12234	missing
12235	duplicate

Task 4

CREDIT NOTES DAY BOOK					
DATE	CLIENT	CREDIT NO	NET £	VAT £	GROSS £
16/5/X0	ROYAL	12233	12.90	2.26	15.16
		12234			
	Duplicate	12235			
	SANDRINGHAM	12236	45.89	8.03	53.92
16/5/X0	TOTAL		58.79	10.29	69.08

ANSWER 41 Main ledger accounts

Sales ledger control account

	£		£
26 April SDB	643.89		

Sales account

	£		£
		26 April SDB	548.01

VAT account

	£		£
		26 April SDB	95.88

Subsidiary ledger accounts

J T Howard			SL15
	£		£
22 April SDB 4671	138.93		

F Parker			SL07
	£		£
22 April SDB 4672	99.07		

Harlow Ltd			SL02
	£		£
23 April SDB 4673	125.10		

	Edmunds & Co		SL13
	£		£
24 April SDB 4674	167.75		

	Peters & Co		SL09
	£		£
26 April SDB 4675	113.04		

ANSWER 42

Sales day book

Date	Invoice No	Customer name	Code	Total	VAT	01	02	03
				£	£	£	£	£
20X0								
6/9	04771	Harold Ellis	H03	93.77	13.96	15.68		64.13
7/9	04772	P Pilot	P01	134.67	20.05		114.62	
	04773	R Tracy	T02	83.30	12.40	23.22	30.80	16.88
8/9	C0612	Harold Ellis	H03	(15.51)	(2.31)			(13.20)
9/9	04774	Planet Inc	P04	165.34	24.62		64.82	75.90
10/9	04775	Harold Ellis	H03	47.23	7.03	23.80	16.40	
	C0613	C Calver	C01	(17.17)	(2.55)	(8.20)		(6.42)
				491.63	73.20	54.50	226.64	137.29

KAPLAN PUBLISHING

Main ledger accounts

Sales ledger control account

	£		£
10/9 SDB	491.63		

Sales – 01

	£		£
		10/9 SDB	54.50

Sales – 02

	£		£
		10/9 SDB	226.64

Sales – 03

	£		£
		10/9 SDB	137.29

VAT account

	£		£
		10/9 SDB	73.20

Subsidiary ledger accounts

Harold Ellis   H03

		£			£
6/9	SDB 04771	93.77	8/9	SDB C0612	15.51
10/9	SDB 04775	47.23			

P Pilot   P01

		£		£
7/9	SDB 04772	134.67		

R Tracy   T02

		£		£
7/9	SDB 04773	83.30		

Planet Inc   P04

		£		£
9/9	SDB 04774	165.34		

C Calver   C01

	£			£
		10/9	SDB C0613	17.17

ANSWER 43

Task 1

<table>
<tr><td colspan="3"></td><td colspan="3" align="center">To be retained by receiving bank</td></tr>
<tr><td colspan="6">For the credit of   Paperbox Ltd</td></tr>
<tr><td colspan="6">Cheques etc for collection to be included in total credit of £ 2,489.87 paid in 19/2/20X0 .</td></tr>
<tr><td></td><td>£</td><td>brought forward</td><td>£1,099.70</td><td>brought forward</td><td>£1,876.81</td></tr>
<tr><td>N J Peal</td><td>291.60</td><td>Pearce & Fellows</td><td>659.18</td><td>R F Wholesalers Ltd</td><td>539.50</td></tr>
<tr><td>Stationery Supplies</td><td>245.30</td><td>Abraham Matthews Ltd</td><td>117.93</td><td></td><td></td></tr>
<tr><td>Candle Company Ltd</td><td>562.80</td><td></td><td></td><td>Credit Card Voucher</td><td>73.56</td></tr>
<tr><td>Carried forward</td><td>£1,099.70</td><td>carried forward</td><td>£1,876.81</td><td>Total cheques etc</td><td>£2,489.87</td></tr>
</table>

Date 19/02/X0

Cashier's stamp and initials

56 – 28 – 48

FINANCIAL BANK PLC

GREENOCK

£50 Notes		
£20 Notes		
£10 Notes		
£5 Notes		
£2 Coins		
£1 Coins		
50p		
20p		
Silver		
Bronze		
Total Cash	-	
Cheques, POs etc	2,489	87
TOTAL £	2,489	87

Fee	No Chqs 6	Paid in by _____
		Address/Ref No. _____

Have you imprinted the summary with your Retailer's Card?

Bank processing copy of Summary
with your Vouchers in correct order:
1 Summary
2 Sales Vouchers
3 Refund Vouchers
Keep Retailer's copy and
     Retailer's Duplicate copy
No more than 200 Vouchers to each Summary
Do not use Staples, Pins, Paper Clips

_____
Retailer's Signature

Complete this summary for every Deposit of Sales Vouchers and enter the
Total on your normal Current Account paying-in slip

	Items	Amount	
Sales vouchers	4	73	56
Less Refund Vouchers			
Date 19/02/X0 Total	£	73 : 56	

Retailer Summary

Retailer's Copy

Retailer Summary

		£	p
Please do not pin or staple	1	22	60
this voucher as this will affect	2	5	83
the machine processing.	3	26	18
	4	18	95
All sales vouchers must be	5		
deposited within three banking	6		
days of the dates shown on them.	7		
	8		
If you are submitting more than 26	9		
vouchers please enclose a separate listing.	10		
	11		
If a voucher contravenes the terms of	12		
the retailer agreement then the amount	13		
shown on the voucher may be charged	14		
back to your bank account, either	15		
direct or via your paying in branch.	16		
	17		
Similarly, if the total amount shown	18		
on the Retail Voucher Summary does	19		
not balance with our total of vouchers, the	20		
difference will be credited (or debited)	21		
to your bank account.	22		
	23		
	24		
	25		
	26		
SALES VOUCHERS TOTAL		73	56

		£	p
	1		
	2		
	3		
	4		
	5		
	6		
	7		
REFUND VOUCHERS TOTAL			

Note re VAT calculations

When recording mail order (cash) sales, the VAT element must be accounted for as this is the first time these sales have been recorded.

Calculation

Amount paid = selling price *including* VAT

Examples

£117.50	=	£100.00	+	£17.50
£100.00	=	£ 85.11	+	£14.89

To calculate VAT element of amount paid:

$$\text{Amount paid} \times \frac{17.5}{117.5}$$

Example

$$£100.00 \times \frac{17.5}{117.5} = £14.89$$

Task 2

Cash Book Receipts

Date	Narrative	Paying-in slip no	Total	Debtors	Mail Order Sales	Other	VAT	Discount allowed
19/2/X0	N J Peal		291.60	291.60				
	Stationery Supplies		245.30	245.30				5.01
	Candle Company Ltd		562.80	562.80				4.95
	Pearce & Fellows		659.18	659.18				13.45
	Abraham Matthews Ltd		117.93	117.93				
	K B Smith		22.60		19.24		3.36	
	R Jones		5.83		4.97		0.86	
	C Bastok		26.18		22.29		3.89	
	J Rirolli		18.95		16.13		2.82	
	R F Wholesalers Ltd (Rent)		539.50			539.50		
	Totals		2,489.87	1,876.81	62.63	539.50	10.93	23.41

Task 3

Code	Account	Debit		Credit	
506	Cash at bank (deposit)				
601	Bank overdraft	2,489	87		
102	Sales mail order			62	63
202	Bank interest				
504	Trade debtors			1,876	81
605	VAT control account			10	93
203	Rent			539	50
409	Discounts allowed	23	41		
504	Trade debtors			23	41
Total		2,513	28	2,513	28

Chapter 13
Credit purchases: documents

ANSWER 44

Credit note from J M Bond & Co

- the trade discount deducted should have been £6.16. Therefore, the total amount of credit is wrong.

ANSWER 45

Invoice from A J Broom & Company Ltd

- 7 joist hangers were invoiced and delivered but only 5 were ordered.

Invoice from Jenson Ltd

- the VAT calculation is incorrect – the amount should be £99.37.

Invoice from Haddow Bros

- 12 sheets were invoiced and ordered but only 10 were delivered.

Chapter 14
Accounting for purchases – summary

ANSWER 46

Purchases day book								
Date	Invoice no	Code	Supplier	Total	VAT	Paint	Wallpaper	Other
22/3/X1	047992	PL03	Mortimer & Co	180.97	26.37		112.00	42.60
	61624	PL06	F L Decor Supplies	64.29	9.57		54.72	
	05531	PL08	Specialist Paint Ltd	219.11	32.21	98.40		88.50
				464.37	68.15	98.40	166.72	131.10

ANSWER 47

JOURNAL ENTRY		No: 0254	
Prepared by:	A N OTHER		
Authorised by:			
Date:	12/3/X1		
Narrative:			
To post the purchases day book to the main ledger			
Account		*Debit*	*Credit*
VAT		184.77	
Purchases – 01		310.76	
Purchases – 02		156.09	
Purchases – 03		245.66	
Purchases – 04		343.43	
Purchases ledger control			1,240.71
TOTALS		1,240.71	1,240.71

Subsidiary ledger

ABG Ltd PL02

		£			£
12/3	PDB CN477	48.31	5/3	Balance b/d	486.90
			10/3	PDB 016127	292.58

Forker & Co PL07

		£			£
10/3	PDB C4366	23.73	5/3	Balance b/d	503.78
			8/3	PDB 11675	207.24

Print Associates PL08

		£			£
			5/3	Balance b/d	229.56
			9/3	PDB 46251	230.04

Homer Ltd PL12

		£			£
			5/3	Balance b/d	734.90
			8/3	PDB 06121	223.87
			11/3	PDB 06132	189.33

		£				£
			5/3	Balance b/d		67.89
			11/3	PDB 77918		169.69

ANSWER 48

Main ledger

Purchases ledger control account

		£				£
			17/2	Balance b/d		2,357.57
			24/2	PDB		942.08

VAT account

		£				£
24/2	PDB	140.30	17/2	Balance b/d		662.47

Purchases – 01 account

		£			£
17/2	Balance b/d	14,275.09			
24/2	PDB	222.05			

Purchases – 02 account

		£			£
17/2	Balance b/d	12,574.26			
24/2	PDB	179.04			

Purchases – 03 account

		£			£
17/2	Balance b/d	29,384.74			
24/2	PDB	302.55			

Purchases – 04 account

		£			£
17/2	Balance b/d	9,274.36			
24/2	PDB	98.14			

Subsidiary ledger

P & F Davis & Co   PL03

		£			£
			17/2	Balance b/d	368.36
			21/2	PDB 46120	166.54
			24/2	PDB 46122	189.23

Clooney & Partner   PL06

		£			£
			17/2	Balance b/d	226.48
			22/2	PDB 46121	230.58

S Doorman   PL07

		£			£
23/2	PDB CN463	21.51	17/2	Balance b/d	218.47
			20/2	PDB 46119	189.53

Fred Janitor   PL11

		£			£
23/2	PDB CN462	30.99	17/2	Balance b/d	111.45
			20/2	PDB 46118	218.70

ANSWER 49

Cash payments book

Date	Details	Cheque no	Code	Total £	VAT £	Purchases ledger £	Cash purchases £	Other £	Discounts received £
8 May	G Rails	001221	PL04	177.56		177.56			4.43
	L Jameson	001222	PL03	257.68		257.68			7.73
	Purchases	001223		216.43	32.23		184.20		
	K Davison	001224	PL07	167.89		167.89			
	T Ives	001225	PL01	289.06		289.06			5.79
	Purchases	001226		263.78	39.28		224.50		
	H Samuels	001227	PL02	124.36		124.36			
				1,496.76	71.51	1,016.55	408.70	-	17.95

JOURNAL ENTRY		No: 1468
Prepared by: A N OTHER		
Authorised by:		

Date:	8 May 20X1		
Narrative:			
To post the cash payments book for the week ending 8 May 20X1			
Account		Debit	Credit
Purchases ledger control		1,016.55	
VAT		71.51	
Purchases		408.70	
Bank			1,496.76
Purchases ledger control		17.95	
Discount received			17.95
TOTALS		1,514.71	1,514.71

Subsidiary ledger

T Ives   PL01

		£			£
8 May	CPB 001225	289.06	1 May	Balance b/d	332.56
8 May	CPB – discount	5.79			

H Samuels   PL02

		£			£
8 May	CPB 001227	124.36	1 May	Balance b/d	286.90

L Jameson   PL03

		£			£
8 May	CPB 001222	257.68	1 May	Balance b/d	623.89
8 May	CPB – discount	7.73			

G Rails   PL04

		£			£
8 May	CPB 001221	177.56	1 May	Balance b/d	181.99
8 May	CPB – discount	4.43			

K Davison   PL07

		£			£
8 May	CPB 001224	167.89	1 May	Balance b/d	167.89

Chapter 15
Petty cash systems

ANSWER 50

Petty cash book

Receipts			Payments								
Date	Narrative	Total £	Date	Narrative	Voucher no	Total £	Postage £	Staff welfare £	Stationery £	Travel expenses £	VAT £
5/1/X1	Bal b/d	150.00	12/1/X1	Postage	03526	13.68	13.68				
				Staff welfare	03527	25.00		25.00			
				Stationery	03528	14.80			12.60		2.20
				Taxi fare	03529	12.00				10.21	1.79
				Staff welfare	03530	6.40		6.40			
				Postage	03531	12.57	12.57				
				Rail fare	03532	6.80				6.80	
				Stationery	03533	7.99			6.80		1.19
				Taxi fare	03534	18.80				16.00	2.80
						118.04	26.25	31.40	19.40	33.01	7.98

CHEQUE REQUISITION FORM

CHEQUE DETAILS

Date .... 12/1/X1 ....

Payee .... Cash ....

Amount £   118.04 ....

Reason ... To restore petty cash ....

Invoice no (attached/to follow) ... - ....

Receipt (attached/to follow) ... - ....

Required by (Print) ...... PETTY CASHIER ....

     (Signature) ...... Petty Cashier ....

Authorised by: ....

Main ledger accounts

Postage account

		£		£
5 Jan	Balance b/d	248.68		
12 Jan	PCB	26.25		

Staff welfare account

		£		£
5 Jan	Balance b/d	225.47		
12 Jan	PCB	31.40		

Stationery account

		£		£
5 Jan	Balance b/d	176.57		
12 Jan	PCB	19.40		

Travel expenses account

		£		£
5 Jan	Balance b/d	160.90		
12 Jan	PCB	33.01		

VAT account

		£			£
12 Jan	PCB	7.98	5 Jan	Balance b/d	2,385.78

ANSWER 51

Voucher total

	£
02634	13.73
02635	8.91
02636	10.57
02637	3.21
02638	11.30
02639	14.66
	62.38

Cash total

		£
£10 note	1	10.00
£5 note	2	10.00
£2 coin	3	6.00
£1 coin	7	7.00
50p coin	5	2.50
20p coin	4	0.80
10p coin	1	0.10
5p coin	2	0.10
2p coin	3	0.06
1p coin	6	0.06
		36.62

Reconciliation of cash and vouchers at 22 May 20X1

	£
Voucher total	62.38
Cash total	36.62
	99.00

The reconciliation shows that there is £1 missing. More cash has been paid out of the petty cash box than is supported by the petty cash vouchers. This could be due to a number of reasons:

- A petty cash claim was made out for, say, £11.30 but mistakenly the amount given to the employee was £12.30.

- An employee borrowed £1 from the petty cash box for business expenses and this has not been recorded on a petty cash voucher.

- £1 has been stolen from the petty cash box.

ANSWER 52

Claimed by	Amount	Comment
J Athersych	£7.04	Valid
J Athersych	£4.85	Valid – less than £5
F Rivers	£12.80	Valid – authorised by department head
M Patterson	£6.60	Cannot be paid – no receipt
D R Ray	£42.80	Cannot be paid – more than £30
J Athersych	£3.70	Valid – less than £5
D R Ray	£12.50	Cannot be paid – not authorised by department head
M Patterson	£19.50	Valid
M T Noble	£17.46	Valid
J Norman	£7.60	Cannot be paid – not authorised by department head

---

ANSWER 53

Petty cash book

Receipts			Payments								
Date	Narrative	Total £	Date	Narrative	Voucher no	Total £	Postage £	Stationery £	Tea & coffee £	Travel £	VAT £
	Bal b/d	100.00	30/4/X1	Coffee/milk	2534	4.68			4.68		
				Postage	2535	13.26	13.26				
				Stationery	2536	10.27		8.74			1.53
				Taxi fare	2537	15.00				12.77	2.23
				Postage	2538	6.75	6.75				
				Train fare	2539	7.40				7.40	
				Stationery	2540	3.86		3.29			0.57
						61.22	20.01	12.03	4.68	20.17	4.33

Main ledger accounts

Postage account

		£		£
23 Apr	Balance b/d	231.67		
30 Apr	PCB	20.01		

Stationery account

		£		£
23 Apr	Balance b/d	334.78		
30 Apr	PCB	12.03		

Tea and coffee account

		£		£
23 Apr	Balance b/d	55.36		
30 Apr	PCB	4.68		

Travel expenses account

		£		£
23 Apr	Balance b/d	579.03		
30 Apr	PCB	20.17		

VAT account

		£			£
30 Apr	PCB	4.33	23 Apr	Balance b/d	967.44

ANSWER 54

TASK 1

Petty cash vouchers which cannot be paid

25/11	Flowers	Receipt required
26/11	VAT book	Authorisation missing
27/11	Rail tickets	Exceeds £100.00 Requires authorisation by MD
30/11	Window cleaner	Uncertainty over coding

TASK 2

The balance of petty cash brought forward can be calculated from the main ledger account or can be assumed to be £100 because the company uses an *imprest system*.

PETTY CASH BOOK

Date	Voucher Number	£		01 Sales £		02 Production £		03 Buying £		04 Finance £		VAT £		Code
30/11/X1	335	13	71					12	21			1	50	0323
	336	3	68							3	68			0424
	337	12	99	12	99									0122
	338	6	78	6	48							0	30	0123
	339	3	51			3	51							0223
	340	6	51							6	51			0423
	Totals	47	18	19	47	3	51	12	21	10	19	1	80	

TASK 3

JOURNAL	PETTY CASH EXPENDITURE		No. *3346*	
Prepared by	*A N Other*	Week ending	*30/11/X1*	
Authorised by				

Department	Expense	Account code	Debit	Credit
Sales / marketing	Entertainment	01 06 01 20		
	Education	21		
	Travelling	22	*12.99*	
	Welfare	23	*6.48*	
	Stationery/Post	24		
Production	Entertainment	01 06 02 20		
	Education	21		
	Travelling	22		
	Welfare	23	*3.51*	
	Stationery/Post	24		
Buying	Entertainment	01 06 03 20		
	Education	21		
	Travelling	22		
	Welfare	23	*12.21*	
	Stationery/Post	24		
Finance	Entertainment	01 06 04 20		
	Education	21		
	Travelling	22		
	Welfare	23	*6.51*	
	Stationery/Post	24	*3.68*	
VAT		02 08 90 00	*1.80*	
Petty cash		01 05 10 00		*47.18*
TOTALS			*47.18*	*47.18*

KAPLAN PUBLISHING

Chapter 16
Bank reconciliations

ANSWER 55

Balance on the cash book

	£
Opening balance	860.40
Add: receipts	5,977.51
Less: payments	(4,029.66)
Closing balance	2,808.25

The amended closing balance on the cash book is £2,808.25 whilst the balance shown on the bank statement is £2,187.15. The difference is due to:

- paying in slips 0065 and 0066 have not yet cleared the banking system;

- cheque numbers 012382, 012385, 012388, 012389 and 012390 have not yet cleared the banking system.

Cash receipts book

Date	Narrative	Total £	VAT £	Debtors £	Other £	Discount £
20X1						
7/3	Paying in slip 0062	1,112.60 ✓	78.80	583.52	450.28	23.60
8/3	Paying in slip 0063	1,047.80 ✓	60.24	643.34	344.22	30.01
9/3	Paying in slip 0064	1,287.64 ✓	71.20	809.59	406.85	34.20
10/3	Paying in slip 0065	987.80	49.90	652.76	285.14	18.03
11/3	Paying in slip 0066	1,127.94	51.84	779.88	296.22	23.12
	BGC – L Fernley	406.90			406.90	
	Bank interest	6.83			6.83	
		5,977.51	311.98	3,875.99	1,789.54	128.96

Cash payments book

Date	Details	Cheque No	Code	Total £	VAT £	Creditors £	Cash purchases £	Other £	Discounts received £
20X1									
7/3	P Barn	012379	PL06	383.21✓		383.21			
	Purchases	012380	ML	268.33✓	39.96		228.37		
	R Trevor	012381	PL12	496.80✓		496.80			6.30
8/3	F Nunn	012382	PL07	218.32		218.32			
	F Taylor	012383	PL09	467.28✓		467.28			9.34
	C Cook	012384	PL10	301.40✓		301.40			
9/3	L White	012385	PL17	222.61		222.61			
	Purchases	012386	ML	269.40✓	40.12		229.28		
	T Finn	012387	PL02	148.60✓		148.60			
10/3	S Penn	012388	PL16	489.23		489.23			7.41
11/3	P Price	012389	PL20	299.99		299.99			
	Purchases	012390	ML	264.49	39.39		225.10		
	Loan Finance	SO	ML	200.00				200.00	
				4,029.66	119.47	3,027.44	682.75	200.00	23.05

KAPLAN PUBLISHING

Bank Statement

FINANCIAL BANK plc CONFIDENTIAL

You can bank on us!

10 Yorkshire Street
Headingley
Leeds LS1 1QT
Telephone: 0113 633061

Account	CURRENT	*Sheet* 00614
Account name	T R FABER	

Statement date **11 March 20X1**   *Account Number* 27943316

Date	Details	Withdrawals (£)	Deposits (£)	Balance (£)
7/3	*Balance from sheet 00613*			860.40
	Bank giro credit L Fernley		406.90	1,267.30
9/3	Cheque 012380	268.33 ✓		
	Cheque 012381	496.80 ✓		
	Credit 0062		1,112.60 ✓	1,614.77
10/3	Cheque 012383	467.28 ✓		
	Cheque 012384	301.40 ✓		
	Credit 0063		1,047.80 ✓	
	SO – Loan Finance	200.00		1,693.89
11/3	Cheque 012379	383.21 ✓		
	Cheque 012386	269.40 ✓		
	Cheque 012387	148.60 ✓		
	Credit 0064		1,287.64 ✓	
	Bank interest		6.83	2,187.15

SO	Standing order	DD	Direct debit	CP	Card purchase
AC	Automated cash	OD	Overdrawn	TR	Transfer

ANSWER 56

Cash book

Receipts		£	Payments		£
16/4	Donald & Co	225.47 ✓	16/4	Balance b/d	310.45
17/4	Harper Ltd	305.68 ✓	17/4	Cheque 03621	204.56
	Fisler Partners	104.67 ✓	18/4	Cheque 03622	150.46 ✓
18/4	Denver Ltd	279.57 ✓	19/4	Cheque 03623	100.80
19/4	Gerald Bros	310.45		Cheque 03624	158.67 ✓
20/4	Johnson & Co	97.68	20/4	Cheque 03625	224.67
			20/4	Balance c/d	173.91
		1,323.52			1,323.52

There are three unticked items on the bank statement:

- Direct debit £183.60 to the District Council;
- Cheque number 03621 £240.56 – this has been entered into the cash book as £204.56;
- Bank interest £3.64.

There are other unticked items in the cash book but these are payments and receipts that have not yet cleared through the banking system.

EXPRESS BANK

CONFIDENTIAL

You can bank on us!

High Street	Account	CURRENT	Sheet 0213
Fenbury			
TL4 6JY	Account name	P L DERBY LTD	
Telephone: 0169 422130			

Statement date   20 April 20X1   Account Number   40429107

Date	Details	Withdrawals (£)	Deposits (£)	Balance (£)
16/4	Balance from sheet 0212			310.45 OD
17/4	DD – District Council	183.60		494.05 OD
18/4	Credit		225.47 ✓	268.58 OD
19/4	Credit		104.67 ✓	
	Cheque 03621	240.56		
	Bank interest	3.64		408.11 OD
20/4	Credit		305.68 ✓	
	Credit		279.57 ✓	
	Cheque 03622	150.46 ✓		
	Cheque 03624	158.67 ✓		131.99 OD

SO	Standing order	DD	Direct debit	CP	Card purchase
AC	Automated cash	OD	Overdrawn	TR	Transfer

ANSWER 57

Graham

Part (a)

Cash account

	£		£
Brought forward	204	Sundry accounts	
Interest on deposit account	18	Standing orders	35
		Bank charges	14
		Carried forward	173
	——		——
	222		222
	——		——
Brought forward	173		

Part (b)

BANK RECONCILIATION STATEMENT AT 31 MARCH 20X3

	£
Balance per bank statement	2,618
Add Uncleared lodgements	723
	——
	3,341
Less Unpresented cheques	(3,168)
	——
Balance per cash account	173
	——

ANSWER 58

BANK RECONCILIATION STATEMENT AS AT 30 JUNE 20X1

	£	£
Balance per bank statement		1,160.25 O/D
Outstanding lodgements:		
30 June		6,910.25
		——————
		5,750.00
Unpresented cheques:		
121	538.00	
122	212.00	
	——————	
		(750.00)
		——————
Balance per cash book		£5,000.00
		——————

ANSWER 59

BANK RECONCILIATION STATEMENT – 31 DECEMBER 20X8

	£
Balance per the cash book	2,381.99
Less items not yet credited	(4,744.66)
	(2,362.67)
Add items not yet debited (800 + 1,436.32 + 9,968.35)	12,204.67
Balance per bank statement	9,842.00

ANSWER 60

TASK 1

Cash book receipts

Date	Narrative	Paying in Slip	Total		Debtors	Mail order	VAT control	Discount allowed
26/6	Trade debtors	598	15,685.23	✓	15,685.23			
	Mail order (Chq/PO)	599	386.29	✓		328.76	57.53	
	Mail order (CC)	600	189.80			76.43	13.37	
27/6	Trade debtors	601	6,650.28	✓	6,650.28			
	Mail order	602	115.98	✓		98.71	17.27	
	Megastores plc	CHAPS	11,755.25	✓	11,755.25			204.17
28/6	Trade debtors	603	12,223.81	✓	12,223.81			
	Mail order	604	609.22	✓		518.49	90.73	
29/6	Trade debtors	605	5,395.40		5,395.40			
	Mail order	606	98.60			83.91	14.69	
30/6	Trade debtors	607	2,641.68		2,641.68			
	Mail Order/shop	608	249.59			212.43	37.16	
29/6	Freeman Foods Group	CHAPS	14,776.04	✓	14,776.04			256.64
30/6	Totals		70,777.17		69,127.69	1,318.73	230.75	460.81

KAPLAN PUBLISHING

Cash book payments

Date	Narrative	Cheque	Total		Creditors	Salaries	Other	VAT control	Discount received
26/6	Blackwood Foodstuffs	389	325.99	✓	325.99				
	Bruning & Soler	390	683.85	✓	683.85				
	Dehlavi Kosmetatos	391	2,112.16	✓	2,112.16				
	Environmentally Friendly Co Ltd	392	705.77		705.77				
	Greig Handling (Import)	393	1,253.98	✓	1,253.98				
	Halpern Freedman	394	338.11	✓	338.11				
	Kobo Design Studio	395	500.00	✓	500.00				
	Rayner Food Co	396	375.22		375.22				
	Year 2000 Produce Co	397	1,100.68		1,100.68				
27/6	HM Customs & Excise	398	23,599.28					23,599.28	
28/6	Salaries - Bank Giro	400	48,995.63			48,995.63			
30/6	Arthur Chong Ltd	401	235.55		235.55				
	Dwyer & Co (Import)	402	469.55		469.55				23.48
	Earthworld Ltd	403	449.28		449.28				22.46
	English Electricity	DD	159.78	✓			135.98	23.80	
	English Telecom	DD	224.47	✓			191.04	33.43	
	Totals		81,529.30		8,550.14	48,995.63	327.02	23,656.51	45.94

Balance on the cash account

	£
Opening balance	84,579.77
Cash book receipts total	70,777.17
Cash book payments total	(81,529.30)
Cash book balance	73,827.64

TASK 2

Main ledger accounts

Sales ledger control account

		£				£
24/6	Balance b/d	312,465.99	30/6	Cash book receipts		69,127.69
			30/6	Cash book receipts - discount		460.81

Mail order sales account

		£				£
			24/6	Balance b/d		26,578.46
			30/6	Cash book receipts		1,318.73

VAT control account

		£				£
30/6	Cash book payments	23,656.51	24/6	Balance b/d		29,375.32
			30/6	Cash book receipts		230.75

Discount allowed account

		£			£
24/6	Balance b/d	4,627.56			
30/6	Cash book receipts	460.81			

Purchases ledger control account

		£			£
30/6	Cash book payments	8,550.14	24/6	Balance b/d	25,476.34
30/6	Cash book payments - discount	45.94			

Salaries account

		£			£
24/6	Balance b/d	105,374.36			
30/6	Cash book payments	48,995.63			

Electricity account

		£			£
24/6	Balance b/d	1,496.57			
30/6	Cash book payments	135.98			

Telephone account

		£			£
24/6	Balance b/d	967.47			
30/6	Cash book payments	191.04			

Discount received account

		£			£
			24/6	Balance b/d	336.58
			30/6	Cash book payments	45.94

TASK 3

FINANCIAL BANK PLC

CONFIDENTIAL

467 HIGH STREET	*Account* **CURRENT**	*Sheet* 455
TAUNTON		
TA1 9WE	*Account name* **NATURAL PRODUCTS LIMITED**	

Telephone
01832 722098

| **20X1** | *Statement date:* | **30 JUNE 20X1** | *Account Number* | 34786695 |

Date	Details		Withdrawals (£)	Deposits (£)	Balance (£)
27 JUN	*Balance from sheet 454*				11,305.11
27 JUN	MEGASTORES PLC	CHAPS		11,755.25✓	
	COUNTER CREDIT 591			13,604.01	
	COUNTER CREDIT 592			112.13	
	374		127.09		
	376	DD	5,955.80		
	ENGLISH ELECTRIC		159.78✓		30,533.83
28 JUN	COUNTER CREDIT 593			11,655.24	
	COUNTER CREDIT 594			683.11	
	COUNTER CREDIT 595			112.19	
	372		87.93		
	389	DD	325.99✓		
	ENGLISH TELECOM		224.47✓		42,345.98
29 JUN	COUNTER CREDIT 596			325.11	
	COUNTER CREDIT 597			60,331.90	
	391		2,112.16✓		
	382		331.80		
	FREEMAN FOODS GRP	CHAPS		14,776.04✓	
	COUNTER CREDIT 598			15,685.23✓	
	COUNTER CREDIT 599			386.29✓	
	COUNTER CREDIT 600			89.80	
	394		338.11✓		
	395		500.00✓		
	386		441.09		
	388		111.94		130,105.25
				6,650.28✓	
30 JUN	COUNTER CREDIT 601			115.98✓	
	COUNTER CREDIT 602		117.54		
	381		3,785.60		
	384		785.11		
	387		683.85✓		
	390		1,253.98✓		
	393		175.10		
	399			12,223.81✓	
	COUNTER CREDIT 603			609.22✓	142,903.36
	COUNTER CREDIT 604				

key	SO *Standing order* DD *Direct debit* CP *Card purchase* AC *Automated cash* OD *Overdrawn*
	CHAPS *Clearing House Automated Payments System* BACS *Bankers Automated Clearing*
Service	

TASK 4

MEMORANDUM

To: *Caroline Everley*
From: *A N Other*
Subject: *Comparison of bank statement and cash book*
Date: *6 July 20X1*

I am enclosing the cash book and bank statement.

When comparing the cash book and the bank statement as at 30 June 20X1 the following errors in the cash book were noted:

Receipt 600 was recorded in the total column of the cash receipts book as £189.80 instead of £89.80. The analysis was recorded as £(76.43 + 13.37) = £89.80.

Cheque number 399 for £175.10 was omitted from the cash book.

TASK 5

Amended cash book balance

	£
Balance per Task 1	73,827.64
Receipt adjustment	(100.00)
Payment omitted	(175.10)
Amended balance	73,552.54

Chapter 17
Ledger balances and control accounts

ANSWER 61

(a) *Subsidiary ledger – sales ledger*

N Pevsner

	£		£
b/f	5,700	c/f	5,850
Sales	150		
	5,850		5,850
b/f	5,850		

R Hackney

	£		£
b/f	5,823	Cash	5,700
Sales	5,280	Bad debt	123
		c/f	5,280
	11,103		11,103
b/f	5,280		

Prince of Wales Hotel

	£		£
b/f	5,826	Cash	5,826
Sales	4,995	c/f	4,995
	10,821		10,821
b/f	4,995		

Subsidiary ledger – purchases ledger

E Lutyens

	£		£
Cash	2,700	b/f	5,481
c/f	5,631	Purchases	2,850
	8,331		8,331
		b/f	5,631

M Hutchinson

	£		£
Cash	150	b/f	5,553
c/f	7,458	Purchases	2,055
	7,608		7,608
		b/f	7,458

H Falkner

	£		£
Cash	2,469	b/f	5,559
c/f	6,450	Purchases	3,360
	8,919		8,919
		b/f	6,450

(b)

Sales ledger control account

	£		£
b/f	17,349	Cash	11,526
Sales	10,425	Bad debts expense written off – R Hackney	123
		c/f	16,125
	27,774		27,774
b/f	16,125		

Purchases ledger control account

	£		£
Cash	5,319	b/f	16,593
c/f	19,539	Purchases	8,265
	24,858		24,858
		b/f	19,539

(c)

Bad debts expense

	£		£
Sales ledger control account (written-off – Hackney)	123		

(d)

List of debtors	£	List of creditors	£
N Pevsner	5,850	E Lutyens	5,631
R Hackney	5,280	M Hutchinson	7,458
Prince of Wales Hotel	4,995	H Falkner	6,450
	16,125		19,539

KAPLAN PUBLISHING

ANSWER 62

(a)

Purchases ledger control account

	£		£
Cash paid	47,028	b/f	5,926
Purchases returns account	202	Purchases (total from PDB)	47,713
Discounts received account	867		
Sales ledger control account (contra)	75		
c/f (bal fig)	5,467		
	53,639		53,639

(b)

Sales ledger control account

	£		£
b/f	10,268	Bank account	69,872
Sales (total from SDB)	71,504	Bad debts account	96
		Sales returns account (total from SRDB)	358
		Discounts allowed (total from discount column in CB)	1,435
		Purchases ledger control account (contra)	75
		c/f (bal fig)	9,936
	81,772		81,772

ANSWER 63

(a)

Purchases ledger control account

	£		£
Cash (2)	1,800	Draft bal b/f	97,186
Contra – sales ledger (3)	1,386	Purchases day book undercast (1)	6,000
Ball c/f	100,000		
	103,186		103,186
		Adjusted bal b/f	100,000

(b) **Reconciliation with list of balances**

	£
Total per list of balances	96,238
Debit balance extracted as a credit (4)	(80)
Balance omitted (5)	3,842
Adjusted balance per control account	100,000

ANSWER 64

(a)

Sales ledger control account

		£			£
30 Sep	b/f	3,825	30 Sep	Bad debts account (2)	400
				Purchases ledger control account (4)	70
				Discount allowed (5)	140
				c/f	3,215
		3,825			3,825
1 Oct	b/f	3,215			

(b) **List of sales ledger balances**

	£
Original total	3,362
Add: Debit balances previously omitted (1)	103
	3,465
Less: Item posted twice to Sparrow's account (3)	(250)
Amended total agreeing with balance on sales ledger control account	3,215

ANSWER 65

(a)

JOURNAL ENTRY		Number:	
Prepared by: A N Other			
Authorised by:			
Date:			
Narrative: To write off bad debt			
Account		*Debit*	*Credit*
Bad debts expense		800.00	
Sales ledger control			800.00
TOTALS		800.00	800.00

(b)

JOURNAL ENTRY		Number:	
Prepared by: A N Other			
Authorised by:			
Date:			
Narrative: To enter contra entry			
Account		Debit	Credit
Purchases ledger control		240.00	
Sales ledger control			240.00
TOTALS		240.00	240.00

(c)

JOURNAL ENTRY		Number:	
Prepared by: A N Other			
Authorised by:			
Date:			
Narrative: To correct undercast of discount allowed			
Account		Debit	Credit
Discount allowed		100.00	
Sales ledger control			100.00
TOTALS		100.00	100.00

ANSWER 66

(a)

JOURNAL ENTRY		Number:	
Prepared by: A N Other			
Authorised by:			
Date:			
Narrative: To correct overcast of purchases day book			
Account		Debit	Credit
Purchases ledger control		1,000.00	
Purchases			1,000.00
TOTALS		1,000.00	1,000.00

(b)

JOURNAL ENTRY	Number:	
Prepared by: A N Other		
Authorised by:		
Date:		
Narrative: To correct posting of discount received		
Account	*Debit*	*Credit*
Purchases ledger control	9.00	
Discount received		9.00
TOTALS	9.00	9.00

(c)

JOURNAL ENTRY	Number:	
Prepared by: A N Other		
Authorised by:		
Date:		
Narrative: To enter contra in main ledger		
Account	*Debit*	*Credit*
Purchases ledger control	300.00	
Sales ledger control		300.00
TOTALS	300.00	300.00

Chapter 18
Drafting an initial trial balance

ANSWER 67

Trial balance at 31 May 20X1

	£	£
Purchases	385,800	
Creditors		32,000
Computer	8,000	
Motor car	19,200	
Discount received		3,850
Telephone	4,320	
Sales returns	6,720	
Wages	141,440	
VAT		7,200
Drawings	60,000	
Discount allowed	6,400	
Rent and rates	26,200	
Debtors	53,500	
Motor expenses	7,700	
Sales		642,080
Stock	38,880	
Inland Revenue		3,800
Purchases returns		2,560
Electricity	6,080	
Bank	1,920	
Capital		74,670
	766,160	766,160

ANSWER 68

Capital account

		£			£
			1 Mar	Bank	12,000

Bank account

		£			£
1 Mar	Capital	12,000	2 Mar	Motor car	4,500
7 Mar	Sales	3,000	2 Mar	Purchases	2,400
20 Mar	Sales	2,100	14 Mar	Rent	600
26 Mar	Debtors	3,800	18 Mar	Stationery	200
			25 Mar	Creditors	3,100
			28 Mar	Drawings	1,600
			31 Mar	Balance c/d	8,500
		20,900			20,900
1 Apr	Balance b/d	8,500			

Motor car account

		£			£
2 Mar	Bank	4,500			

Purchases account

		£			£
2 Mar	Bank	2,400			
4 Mar	Creditors	2,500			
12 Mar	Creditors	4,100	31 Mar	Balance c/d	9,000
		9,000			9,000
1 Apr	Balance b/d	9,000			

Creditors' account

		£			£
25 Mar	Bank	3,100	4 Mar	Purchases	2,500
31 Mar	Balance c/d	3,500	12 Mar	Purchases	4,100
		6,600			6,600
			1 Apr	Balance b/d	3,500

Sales account

		£			£
			7 Mar	Bank	3,000
			10 Mar	Debtors	4,600
			15 Mar	Debtors	3,500
31 Mar	Balance c/d	13,200	20 Mar	Bank	2,100
		13,200			13,200
			1 Apr	Balance b/d	13,200

Debtors' account

		£			£
10 Mar	Sales	4,600	26 Mar	Bank	3,800
15 Mar	Sales	3,500	31 Mar	Balance c/d	4,300
		8,100			8,100
1 Apr	Balance b/d	4,300			

Rent account

		£			£
14 Mar	Bank	600			

Stationery account

		£			£
18 Mar	Bank	200			

Drawings account

		£			£
28 Mar	Bank	1,600			

Trial balance at 31 March

	£	£
Capital		12,000
Bank	8,500	
Motor car	4,500	
Purchases	9,000	
Creditors		3,500
Sales		13,200
Debtors	4,300	
Rent	600	
Stationery	200	
Drawings	1,600	
	28,700	28,700

ANSWER 69

Trial balance at 30 June 20X1

	£	£
Debtors	33,440	
Bank	1,200	
Sales		401,300
Stock	24,300	
Wages	88,400	
Telephone	2,700	
Motor car	12,000	
VAT		7,000
Electricity	3,800	
Rent	16,400	
Purchases	241,180	
Purchases returns		1,600
Sales returns	4,200	
Office equipment	5,000	
Capital		49,160
Motor expenses	4,840	
Discounts allowed	4,010	
Discounts received		2,410
Creditors		20,000
Drawings	40,000	
	481,470	481,470

ANSWER 70

TASKS 1 TO 3

Main ledger

Sales ledger control account

Date	Details	Amount	Date	Details	Amount
		£			£
Dec 1	Balance b/d	537,483	Dec 1	Sales returns DB	167
	Sales DB	24,587		Bank	1,755
	Bank	1,000		Discounts	45
			Dec 1	Balance c/d	561,103
		_____			_____
		563,070			563,070
		_____			_____
Dec 2	Balance b/d	561,103			

Purchases ledger control account

Date	Details	Amount	Date	Details	Amount
		£			£
Dec 1	Purchases returns DB	32	Dec 1	Balance b/d	404,546
	Bank	14,953		Purchases DB	29,310
	Discounts	112			
Dec 1	Balance c/d	418,759			
		_____			_____
		433,856			433,856
		_____			_____
			Dec 2	Balance b/d	418,759

Equipment

Date	Details	Amount	Date	Details	Amount
		£			£
Dec 1	Balance b/d	4,182	Dec 1	Balance c/d	5,008
	Bank	826			
		_____			_____
		5,008			5,008
		_____			_____
Dec 2	Balance b/d	5,008			

Heating and lighting

Date	Details	Amount	Date	Details	Amount
		£			£
Dec 1	Balance b/d	1,728	Dec 1	Balance c/d	2,244
	Purchases DB	516			
		_____			_____
		2,244			2,244
		_____			_____
Dec 2	Balance b/d	2,244			

Purchases

Date	Details	Amount	Date	Details	Amount
		£			£
Dec 1	Balance b/d	2,432,679	Dec 1	Balance c/d	2,457,304
	Purchases DB	24,429			
	Bank	196			
		_____			_____
		2,457,304			2,457,304
		_____			_____
Dec 2	Balance b/d	2,457,304			

VAT

Date	Details	Amount	Date	Details	Amount
		£			£
Dec 1	Purchases DB	4,365	Dec 1	Balance b/d	63,217
	Sales returns DB	25		Sales DB	3,662
	Bank	193		Purchases returns DB	5
Dec 1	Balance c/d	62,301			
		66,884			66,884
			Dec 2	Balance b/d	62,301

Subsidiary (sales) ledger

Classic Music

Date	Details	Amount	Date	Details	Amount
		£			£
Dec 1	Balance b/d	16,742	Dec 1	Sales returns DB	167
	Sales DB	1,978		Bank	1,755
	Bank	1,000		Discount allowed	45
			Dec 1	Balance c/d	17,753
		19,720			19,720
Dec 2	Balance b/d	17,753			

Subsidiary (purchases) ledger

Atlantic Imports Ltd

Date	Details	Amount	Date	Details	Amount
		£			£
Dec 1	Purchases returns DB	32	Dec 1	Balance b/d	43,607
	Bank	4,388		Purchases DB	12,528
	Discount received	112			
Dec 1	Balance c/d	51,603			
		56,135			56,135
			Dec 2	Balance b/d	51,603

TASK 4

List of updated balances

	Debit balances £	Credit balances £
Customers:		
Hit Records Ltd (10,841 + 4,279)	15,120	
Smiths & Co (18,198 + 6,023)	24,221	
Classic Music	17,753	
Other customers (491,702 + 12,307)	504,009	
Suppliers:		
HMI Ltd (82,719 + 10,524)		93,243
Atlantic Imports Ltd		51,603
Southern Electric (NIL + 606)		606
Other suppliers (278,220 + 5,652 – 10,565)		273,307
Purchases	2,457,304	
Sales (3,284,782 + 20,925)		3,305,707
Sales returns (10,973 + 142)	11,115	
Purchases returns (9,817 + 27)		9,844
Heating and lighting	2,244	
Equipment	5,008	
Equipment repairs (166 + 102 – 15)	253	
Bank charges (82 + 67)	149	
VAT		62,301
Bank		1,075
Discount allowed (11,420 + 45)	11,465	
Discount received (8,516 + 112)		8,628
Other debit balances	1,368,815	
Other credit balances		611,142
Totals	4,417,456	4,417,456

Chapter 19
Final Accounts and Accounting Concepts

ANSWER 71

J Risdon Trading and Profit and Loss Account for year ended 31 March 2007

	£	£
Sales (work done)		84,500
Opening Stock		
Materials	1,750	
Add Purchases	38,100	
	39,850	
Less stocks at 31 March 2007-07-30	(1,850)	
Cost of Materials Used	38,000	
Gross Profit		46,500
Expenses		
Repairs and Maintenance	1,750	
Motor Vehicle Running Cost	4,100	
Insurance	1,400	
Office Expenses	700	
Wages	8,750	
		16,700
Net profit for year		29,800

Balance Sheet as at 31 March 2007

	£	£
Fixed Assets		
Tools and Equipment	20,000	
Motor Vehicles	18,500	
Office Equipment	5,000	
		43,500
Current Assets		
Stocks	1,850	
Debtors	4,100	
Bank	4,000	
Cash	450	
	10,400	
Less Current Liabilities		
Creditors	2,600	
VAT	1,000	
	3,600	
Net Current Assets		6,800
Total Assets Less Current Liabilities		50,300
Less Long Term Liabilities		
Loan		6,500
		43,800
Financed by:-		
Capital		36,000
Add profit for year		29,800
		65,800
Less Drawings		22,000
		43,800

KAPLAN PUBLISHING

ANSWER 72

Andrew Fewster, Trading and Profit and Loss Account for year ended 31 March 2007

	£	£
Sales (work done)		86,500
Opening stock		
Materials	1,950	
Add Purchases	39,500	
	41,450	
Less Stocks at 31 March 2007-07-30	2,150	
Cost of Materials used	39,300	
Gross Profit		47,200
Expenses		
Repairs to Hallways	1,950	
Motor Vehicle Running Costs	4,250	
Insurance (1850 – 250)	1,600	
Office Expenses (950 -150)	1,000	
Wages	9,200	
Depreciation Motor Vehicles	5,625	
Depreciation Tools & Equipment	5,250	
Depreciation Office Equipment	1,375	
		30,250
Net profit for year		16,950

Balance Sheet as at 31 March 2007

	£	£
Fixed Assets NBV		
Motor Vehicle		16,875
Tools & Equipment		15,750
Office Equipment		4,125
		36,750
Current Assets		
Stocks	2,150	
Debtors	5,500	
Pre-Payments	250	
Bank	1,000	
Cash	200	
	9,100	
Less Current Liabilities		
Creditors	2,950	
Accruals	50	
VAT	1,400	
	4,400	
Net current assets		4,700
Total assets less current liabilities		41,450
Less Long Term Liabilities		
Bank loan		10,500
		30,950
Financed by:-		
Capital		37,500
Net profit for year		16,950
		54,450
Less drawings		23,500
		30,950

KAPLAN PUBLISHING

Chapter 20

Capital expenditure and revenue expenditure

ANSWER 73

Stapling machine

(a)   No.

(b)   Although, by definition, since the stapler will last a few years, it might seem to be a fixed asset, its treatment would come within the remit of the concept of materiality and would probably be treated as office expenses.

ANSWER 74

Office equipment

The item will have value in future years and could therefore be regarded as fixed assets. However, the stronger argument is that this is not justified by the relatively small amount involved and the concept of materiality would suggest treatment as an expense of the year.

ANSWER 75

Engine

Revenue expenditure. This is a repair rather than an improvement to an asset. It maintains the level of operation, rather than increasing it.

ANSWER 76

When the first instalment is paid.

Chapter 21
Depreciation

ANSWER 77

Motor car - cost account

		£			£
20X3			20X3		
1 Jan	Purchase ledger control	12,000	31 Dec	Balance c/d	12,000
20X4			20X4		
1 Jan	Balance b/d	12,000	31 Dec	Balance c/d	12,000
20X5			20X5		
1 Jan	Balance b/d	12,000	31 Dec	Balance c/d	12,000
20X6					
1 Jan	Balance b/d	12,000			

$$\text{Annual depreciation charge} = \frac{12,000 - 2,400}{4}$$

$$= £2,400$$

Motor car – provision for depreciation account

		£			£
20X3			20X3		
31 Dec	Balance c/d	2,400	31 Dec	Depreciation expense	2,400
			20X4		
20X4			1 Jan	Balance b/d	2,400
31 Dec	Balance c/d	4,800	31 Dec	Depreciation expense	2,400
		4,800			4,800
			20X5		
			1 Jan	Balance b/d	4,800
20X5			31 Dec	Depreciation expense	2,400
31 Dec	Balance c/d	7,200			
		7,200			7,200
			20X6		
			1 Jan	Balance b/d	7,200

Depreciation (profit and loss) account

	£		£
20X3		**20X3**	
31 Dec Motor car provision for depreciation	2,400	31 Dec P&L a/c	2,400
20X4		**20X4**	
31 Dec Motor car provision for depreciation	2,400	31 Dec P&L a/c	2,400
20X5		**20X5**	
31 Dec Motor car provision for depreciation	2,400	31 Dec P&L a/c	2,400

ANSWER 78

(1)   Straight line method

$$\text{Annual depreciation} = \frac{\text{Cost - Scrap value}}{\text{Estimated life}}$$

$$= \frac{£6,000 - £1,000}{8 \text{ years}}$$

$$= £625 \text{ pa}$$

Machine account

	£		£
Year 1:			
Cost	6,000		

Provision for depreciation

	£		£
Year 1:		Year 1:	
Balance c/d	625	Depreciation expense	625
Year 2:		Year 2:	
		Balance b/d	625
Balance c/d	1,250	Depreciation expense	625
	1,250		1,250
Year 3:		Year 3:	
		Balance b/d	1,250
Balance c/d	1,875	Depreciation expense	625
	1,875		1,875
		Year 4:	
		Balance b/d	1,875

Balance sheet extract:

		Cost £	Accumulated depreciation £	Net book value £
Fixed asset:				
Year 1	Machine	6,000	625	5,375
Year 2	Machine	6,000	1,250	4,750
Year 3	Machine	6,000	1,875	4,125

(2)   Reducing balance method

		£
Cost		6,000
Year 1	Depreciation 20% × £6,000	1,200
		4,800
Year 2	Depreciation 20% × £4,800	960
		3,840
Year 3	Depreciation 20% × £3,840	768
Net book value		3,072

ANSWER 79   Hillton

Part (a)

Workings

		Chopper £	Mincer £	Stuffer £	Total £
Cost		4,000	6,000	8,000	18,000
Depreciation	20X6 – 25%	(1,000)			(1,000)
Depreciation	20X7 – 25%	(1,000)	(1,500)		(2,500)
Depreciation	20X8 – 25%	(1,000)	(1,500)	(2,000)	(4,500)
Net book value at 31 Dec 20X8		1,000	3,000	6,000	10,000

Machinery

	£		£
20X6		**20X6**	
Cash – chopper	4,000	Balance c/d	4,000
20X7		**20X7**	
Balance b/d	4,000		
Cash – mincer	6,000	Balance c/d	10,000
	10,000		10,000
20X8		**20X8**	
Balance b/d	10,000		
Cash – stuffer	8,000	Balance c/d	18,000
	18,000		18,000
20X9			
Balance b/d	18,000		

Provision for depreciation (machinery)

	£		£
20X6		**20X6**	
		Depreciation expense	
Balance c/d	1,000	(25% × £4,000)	1,000
	———		———
20X7		**20X7**	
Balance c/d	3,500	Balance b/d	1,000
		Depreciation expense	
		(25% × £10,000)	2,500
	———		———
	3,500		3,500
	———		———
20X8		**20X8**	
Balance c/d	8,000	Balance b/d	3,500
		Depreciation expense	
		(25% × £18,000)	4,500
	———		———
	8,000		8,000
	———		———
		20X9	
		Balance b/d	8,000

Depreciation expense (machinery)

	£		£
20X6		**20X6**	
Provision for depreciation	1,000	Profit and loss account	1,000
	———		———
20X7		**20X7**	
Provision for depreciation	2,500	Profit and loss account	2,500
	———		———
20X8		**20X8**	
Provision for depreciation	4,500	Profit and loss account	4,500
	———		———

Part (b)

Workings

		Metro £	Transit £	Astra £	Total £
Cost		3,200	6,000	4,200	13,400
Depreciation	20X6 – 40%	(1,280)			(1,280)
		———			———
NBV 31.12.X6		1,920			
Depreciation	20X7 – 40%	(768)	(2,400)		(3,168)
		———			———
NBV 31.12.X7		1,152	3,600		
Depreciation	20X8 – 40%	(461)	(1,440)	(1,680)	(3,581)
		———	———	———	———
Net book value at 31 Dec 20X8		691	2,160	2,520	5,371
		———	———	———	———

Motor vehicles

	£		£
20X6		**20X6**	
Cash – Metro	3,200	Balance c/d	3,200
20X7		**20X7**	
Balance b/d	3,200		
Cash – Transit	6,000	Balance c/d	9,200
	9,200		9,200
20X8		**20X8**	
Balance b/d	9,200		
Cash – Astra	4,200	Balance c/d	13,400
	13,400		13,400
20X9			
Balance b/d	13,400		

Provision for depreciation (motor vehicles)

	£		£
20X6		**20X6**	
		Depreciation expense	
Balance c/d	1,280	(40% × £3,200)	1,280
20X7		**20X7**	
Balance c/d	4,448	Balance b/d	1,280
		Depreciation expense	
		(40% × (£9,200 - £1,280))	3,168
	4,448		4,448
20X8		**20X8**	
Balance c/d	8,029	Balance b/d	4,448
		Depreciation expense	
		(40% × (£13,400 - £4,448))	3,581
	8,029		8,029
		20X9	
		Balance b/d	8,029

Depreciation expense (motor vehicles)

	£		£
20X6		**20X6**	
Provision for depreciation	1,280	Profit and loss account	1,280
20X7		**20X7**	
Provision for depreciation	3,168	Profit and loss account	3,168
20X8		**20X8**	
Provision for depreciation	3,581	Profit and loss account	3,581

KAPLAN PUBLISHING

ANSWER 80

	£
Depreciation for vehicle sold 1 March 20X3	900
Depreciation for vehicle purchased 1 June 20X3	1,000
Depreciation for vehicle purchased 1 September 20X3	600
Depreciation for other vehicles owned during the year	2,080
Total depreciation for the year ended 30 November 20X3	4,580

Chapter 22

Accruals and prepayments

ANSWER 81

Siobhan

Rent payable

	£		£
Cash paid	15,000	P&L account	12,000
		Carried forward	3,000
	15,000		15,000
Brought forward (prepayment)	3,000		

Gas

	£		£
Cash paid	840	P&L account	1,440
Carried forward	600		
	1,440		1,440
		Brought forward (accrual)	600

Advertising

	£		£
Cash	3,850	P&L account	3,350
		Carried forward	500
	3,850		3,850
Brought forward (prepayment)	500		

Bank interest

	£		£
Cash	28	P&L account	96
Cash	45		
Carried forward ($\frac{1}{3} \times 69$)	23		
	96		96
		Brought forward (accrual)	23

Rates

	£		£
Brought forward (prepayment $\frac{3}{6} \times 4{,}800$)	2,400	P&L account	11,300
Cash	5,600		
Carried forward ($\frac{3}{6} \times 6{,}600$)	3,300		
	11,300		11,300
		Brought forward (accrual)	3,300

Rent receivable

	£		£
Brought forward (debtor = accrued income)	125	Cash	250
P&L account (W)	575	Cash	600
Carried forward ($\frac{3}{12} \times 600$)	150		
	850		850
		Brought forward (creditor = deferred income)	150

Working

Profit and loss account credit for rent receivable

	£
1 January 20X4 – 31 March 20X4 ($\frac{3}{6} \times 250$)	125
1 April 20X4 – 31 December 20X4 ($\frac{9}{12} \times 600$)	450
	575

ANSWER 82

A Crew

Stationery

		£			£
31 Dec	Balance per trial balance	560	31 Dec	P&L account	545
			31 Dec	C/f (prepayment)	15
		———			———
		560			560
		———			———
1 Jan	Brought forward	15			

Rent

		£			£
31 Dec	Balance per trial balance	900	31 Dec	P&L account	1,200
31 Dec	Carried forward (accrual)	300			
		———			———
		1,200			1,200
		———			———
			1 Jan	Brought forward	300

Rates

		£			£
31 Dec	Balance per trial balance	380	31 Dec	P&L account	310
			31 Dec	C/f (prepayment)	70
		———			———
		380			380
		———			———
1 Jan	Brought forward	70			

Lighting and heating

		£			£
31 Dec	Balance per trial balance	590	31 Dec	P&L account	605
31 Dec	Carried forward (accrual)	15			
		———			———
		605			605
		———			———
			1 Jan	Brought forward	15

Insurance

		£			£
31 Dec	Balance per trial balance	260	31 Dec	P&L account	190
			31 Dec	C/f (prepayment)	70
		———			———
		260			260
		———			———
1 Jan	Brought forward	70			

Wages and salaries

		£			£
31 Dec	Balance per trial balance	2,970	31 Dec	P&L account	2,970
		———			———

ANSWER 83

A Metro

Motor tax and insurance

	£		£
Brought forward	570	P&L account (W2)	2,205
Cash		Carried forward (W1)	835
1 April	420		
1 May	1,770		
1 July	280		
	3,040		3,040
Brought forward	835		

Workings

1   *Prepayment at the end of the year*

	£
Motor tax on six vans paid 1 April 20X0 ($\frac{3}{12} \times 420$)	105
Insurance on ten vans paid 1 May 20X0 ($\frac{4}{12} \times 1{,}770$)	590
Motor tax on four vans paid 1 July 20X0 ($\frac{6}{12} \times 280$)	140
Total prepayment	835

2   *Profit and loss charge for the year*

There is no need to calculate this as it is the balancing figure, but it could be calculated as follows.

	£
Prepayment	570
Motor tax ($\frac{9}{12} \times 420$)	315
Insurance ($\frac{8}{12} \times 1{,}770$)	1,180
Motor tax ($\frac{6}{12} \times 280$)	140
Profit and loss charge	2,205

Chapter 23
VAT

ANSWER 84

VAT records – checklist

The form of records must be such that the Customs and Excise can check VAT returns easily.

A business must keep a record of:

- all taxable and exempt supplies made in the course of business.
- all taxable supplies received in the course of business.
- a summary of total output tax and input tax for each period – the VAT account.

The business must keep records to verify figures shown on VAT returns for the previous six years.

These might include:

- Orders and delivery notes
- Business correspondence
- Appointment and job books
- Purchases and sales books
- Cash books and other account books.
- Copy purchase and sales invoices.
- Record of daily takings including till rolls.
- Import and export documents.
- VAT accounts
- Credit notes, issued and received.

ANSWER 85

VAT terminology definitions

- Supply of goods – the passing of exclusive ownership of goods to another person.
- Supply of services – doing something, other than supplying goods, for consideration.
- Output tax – tax collected from customers and clients.
- Input tax – tax paid to suppliers of goods and services.
- Zero-rated item – these relate to specific items listed in the VAT Act 1994 (eg food).
- Exempt item – specific items listed in the VAT Act 1994 (eg education).
- Standard rated – items which are not zero-rated, taxable at the reduced rate (eg domestic fuel and power), or exempt from VAT.

ANSWER 86

Invoices must show (unless it is a less detailed tax invoice) the following:

- Identification number
- Date of supply (the 'tax point')
- Date of issue of the invoice
- Supplier's name and address and VAT registration number
- Name and address of customer
- Type of supply, eg sale, hire
- Description of the goods or services supplied
- Quantity of goods or extent of service rendered
- Rate of tax and amount payable for each item excluding tax

- Total amount payable (excluding tax)
- Rate of any cash discount
- Amount of tax chargeable
- Separate rate and tax charged for each rate of VAT

ANSWER 87

Less detailed tax invoice

Retailers often take advantage of this facility.

Where the tax-inclusive price does not exceed £100, a retailer may issue a 'less detailed tax invoice'.

It must contain the following elements:

- Supplier's name and address
- Supplier's VAT number
- Date of supply
- Description of goods
- Amount payable including VAT
- Rate of VAT

NB: All retailers must keep a record of their daily gross takings so that the output tax can be determined.

KAPLAN PUBLISHING

ANSWER 88

Value Added Tax Return

For Official Use

For the period

01/04/X1 to 30/06/X1

Registration number	Period
131 7250 19	06 X1

HM Customs
and Excise

Duncan Bye
Low House
Low Green
Derbyshire
DE1 7XU   140784/06

You could be liable to a financial penalty if your completed return and all the VAT payable are not received by the due date.

Due date: 31.07.X1

For
official
use

Your VAT Office telephone number is 0151 644211

If you may trade or pay taxes in euro from Jan 1999. Contact your Business Advice Centre for C&E queries or Treasury Enquiry Unit on 0171 270 4558

Before you fill in this form read the notes on the back and the VAT leaflet *'Filling in your VAT Return'*. Fill in all boxes clearly in ink, and write 'none' where necessary. Don't put a dash or leave any box blank. If there are no pence write '**00**' in the pence column. **Do not** enter more than one amount in any box.

For official use		£	P
	VAT due in this period on **sales** and other outputs	3,783	50
	VAT due in this period on **acquisitions** from other **EC Member States**	None	
	Total VAT due (**the sum of boxes 1 and 2**)	3,783	50
	VAT reclaimed in this period on **purchases** and other inputs (including acquisitions from the EC)	1,605	73
		2,177	27
	Total value of **sales** and all other outputs excluding any VAT. **Include your box 8 figure.**	21,620	00
	Total value of **purchases** and all other inputs excluding any VAT. **Include your box 9 figure.**	9,176	00
	Total value of all **supplies** of goods and related services, excl any VAT, to other **EC Member States.**	None	00
	Total value of all **acquisitions** of goods and related servs, excl any VAT, from other **EC Member States.**	None	00

Retail schemes. If you have used any of the schemes in the period covered by this return, enter the relevant letter(s) in this box.

If you are enclosing a payment please tick this box.

DECLARATION: You, or someone on your behalf, must sign below.

I, ... DUNCAN BYE .... declare that the

(Full name of signatory in BLOCK LETTERS)

information given above is true and complete.

Signature.. Date .... 19............

A false declaration can result in prosecution.

0141846

VAT 100 (Full)   PCU (June 1996)   F

ANSWER 89

Task 1

<table>
<tr><td colspan="3" align="center">**Value Added Tax Return**

For the period

01/07/X1 to 30/09/X1</td><td colspan="2">For Official Use</td></tr>
</table>

HM Customs and Excise

Value Added Tax Return

For the period

01/07/X1 to 30/09/X1

For Official Use

Registration number	Period
123 9872 17	09 X1

You could be liable to a financial penalty if your completed return and all the VAT payable are not received by the due date.

Due date: 31 10 X1

For official use

Mark Ambrose

High Park House

High Melton

Your VAT Office telephone number is 0151 644211

ATTENTION

If you may trade or pay taxes in euro from Jan 1999, Contact your Business Advice Centre for C&E queries or Treasury Enquiry Unit on 020 7270 4558

Before you fill in this form read the notes on the back and the VAT leaflet *'Filling in your VAT Return'*. Fill in all boxes clearly in ink, and write 'none' where necessary. Don't put a dash or leave any box blank. If there are no pence write '**00**' in the pence column. **Do not** enter more than one amount in any box.

For official use				£	P
	VAT due in this period on **sales** and other outputs	1		6,807	50
	VAT due in this period on **acquisitions** from other **EC Member States**	2		None	
	Total VAT due (**the sum of boxes 1 and 2**)	3		6,807	50
	VAT reclaimed in this period on **purchases** and other inputs (including acquisitions from the EC)	4		2,999	50
	Net VAT to be paid to Customs or reclaimed by you (Difference between boxes 3 and 4)	5		3,808	00
	Total value of **sales** and all other outputs excluding any VAT. **Include your box 8 figure.**	6		38,900	00
	Total value of **purchases** and all other inputs excluding any VAT. **Include your box 9 figure.**	7		16,740	00
	Total value of all **supplies** of goods and related services. excl any VAT. to other **EC Member States.**	8		None	00
	Total value of all **acquisitions** of goods and related servs. excl any VAT. from other **EC Member States.**	9		None	00

Retail schemes. If you have used any of the schemes in the period covered by this return, enter the relevant letter(s) in this box.

If you are enclosing a payment please tick this box.	DECLARATION: You, or someone on your behalf, must sign below. I, ... MARK AMBROSE .... declare that the (Full name of signatory in BLOCK LETTERS) information given above is true and complete. Signature... Date ....20..............

VAT 100 (Full)   0141846

PCU (June 1996)

F

DANIEL AND JAMES

LICENSED BOOKKEEPERS

Stonehill House
Stonehill Rise
Doncaster
DN5 9HB

Tel/Fax: 01302 786050

e-mail: danjames@virgin.net

25 October 20X1

Dear Mr Ambrose

Re: VAT return quarter ended 30 September 20X1

I enclose your completed VAT form for signature and submission to the Customs and Excise. You need to pay £3,808 for this period.

I have adjusted your output and input tax for the quarter to take account of both the bad debt relief and the goods for own use. Relief can be claimed on bad debts which are over six months old at the date of the return. I have therefore adjusted your input tax by £70, being bad debt relief claimed on both High Melton Farms and Concorde Motors. The bad debt relief for Bawtry Engineering will be claimed next quarter.

The use of materials for private purposes has to be treated as an output and attracts VAT on the cost of the items. I have therefore added a further £87.50 to your output tax for the period, to account for this item, which will be treated as drawings when your accounts are drafted.

If you wish to raise any of the issues above with me, please don't hesitate to give me a call.

Yours sincerely

A Bookkeeper

| **Partners:** | James Musgrave |
| | Daniel Robb |

Workings for VAT return

		£
Box 1 :	From SDB	6,720.00
	Goods for own use	87.50
		6,807.50
Box 4 :	From PDB	2,882.25
	Petty cash	47.25
	Bad debts	70.00
		2,999.50

Task 1

<table>
<tr><td colspan="2">

Value Added Tax Return

For the period

01/07/X1 to 30/09/X1

HM Customs
and Excise

John Thistle
t/as Crescent Hotel
High Street
Whitby
YO21 37L   140784/06

Your VAT Office telephone number is 0151 644211

</td><td>

For Official Use

Registration number	Period
179 6421 27	09 X1

You could be liable to a financial penalty if your completed return and all the VAT payable are not received by the due date.

Due date: 31.10.X1

For official use	

ATTENTION

If you may trade or pay taxes in euro from Jan 1999, Contact your Business Advice Centre for C&E queries or Treasury Enquiry Unit on 020 7270 4558

</td></tr>
</table>

Before you fill in this form read the notes on the back and the VAT leaflet *'Filling in your VAT Return'*. Fill in all boxes clearly in ink, and write 'none' where necessary. Don't put a dash or leave any box blank. If there are no pence write '00' in the pence column. **Do not** enter more than one amount in any box.

For official use			£	p
	VAT due in this period on **sales** and other outputs	1	14,455	00
	VAT due in this period on **acquisitions** from other **EC Member States**	2	None	
	Total VAT due (**the sum of boxes 1 and 2**)	3	14,455	00
	VAT reclaimed in this period on **purchases** and other inputs (including acquisitions from the EC)	4	4,942	00
	Net VAT to be paid to Customs or reclaimed by you (Difference between boxes 3 and 4)	5	9,513	00
	Total value of **sales** and all other outputs excluding any VAT. **Include your box 8 figure.**	6	82,600	00
	Total value of **purchases** and all other inputs excluding any VAT. **Include your box 9 figure.**	7	27,740	00
	Total value of all **supplies** of goods and related services, excl any VAT, to other **EC Member States.**	8	None	00
	Total value of all **acquisitions** of goods and related servs, excl any VAT, from other **EC Member States.**	9	None	00

Retail schemes. If you have used any of the schemes in the period covered by this return, enter the relevant letter(s) in this box.

If you are enclosing a payment please tick this box.	DECLARATION: You, or someone on your behalf, must sign below.
	I, ...JOHN THISTLE.. declare that the (Full name of signatory in BLOCK LETTERS) information given above is true and complete. Signature.. Date ....20............. **A false declaration can result in prosecution.**

VAT 100 (Full)   0141846

PCU (June 1996)   F

Task 2

NOTE

To: John Thistle

From: Simon White

Date: 18 October 20X1

I have completed the VAT return for the quarter ended 30 September ready for your signature.

I have made adjustments to account for both the bad debt written off and the goods for own use.

The VAT element of the bad debt, £87.50, has been added to the input tax for the period.

The VAT element on the goods at cost, £52.50, has been added to the output tax as the £300 is treated as an output.

The £352.50 will be charged to your drawings account.

Task 3

Simon White
Bookkeeper
Bay Farm
High Street
Hawsker
YO21 3EJ

Date: 22 October 20X1

VAT Office
Customs House
Bright Street
Scarborough
YO33 23J

Dear Sirs

Re: Special Retail Schemes

One of my clients is planning to purchase a retail business.

I understand that there are special VAT schemes that apply to such businesses.

Could you please send me any relevant information or standard publications you have which cover this matter.

Yours faithfully

S White

Workings for VAT return

		£
Box 1 :	From SDB	9,642.50
	From cash takings	4,760.00
	Goods for own use	52.50
		14,455.00
Box 4 :	From PDB	2,892.75
	Bar and restaurant	1,890.00
	Petty cash	71.75
	Bad debt	87.50
		4,942.00